The First Years of Forever

ED WHEAT, M.D.

with Gloria Okes Perkins

ZONDERVAN™

GRAND RAPIDS, MICHIGAN 49530

ZONDERVAN™

The First Years of Forever
Copyright © 1988 by Ed Wheat

Requests for information should be addressed to:
Zondervan, *Grand Rapids, Michigan 49530*

Library of Congress Cataloging-in-Publication Data

Wheat, Ed.
 The first years of forever / Ed Wheat.
 ISBN 0-310-42531-X
 1. Marriage—United States. 2. Marriage—Religious aspects—Christianity.
I. Perkins, Gloria Okes. II. Title.
 HQ734.W518 1988
 3M306.8'1   88-20778

The case studies in this book are true. The names have been changed except for the references to the author.

Edited by Nia Jones
Interior design by Nia Jones
Cover design by Cindy Davis
Cover photo by Comstock, Inc.
Printed in the United States of America

06 07 08 /❖ DC/ 27 26 25 24 23 22

With thanksgiving for
our wonderful marriage partners,
Gaye and Dan,
whose love and encouragement
shine through every page of this book.

CONTENTS

Preface

Readers who are familiar with the byline Ed Wheat, M. D. and Gaye Wheat will note another name on this volume, which rightly belongs on all our books. For the past ten years we have had the privilege of working closely with Gloria Okes Perkins, a gifted professional writer and biblical counselor. The result has been *Intended for Pleasure,* which has found its place as the standard reference book for Christians concerned with sex in marriage from the medical and biblical perspectives; *LOVE LIFE,* the Zondervan book that has been read by more than half a million couples seeking to rekindle love in their marriage; and *How To Save Your Marriage Alone,* the little book in large demand by individuals facing the personal threat of divorce. Together, Gloria and I have also produced a videocassette series of premarriage counseling albums and three counseling cassettes, including "Before the Wedding Night, " which is the forerunner of *The First Years of Forever.*

Since the Lord brought Gloria and her husband, Dan, to northwest Arkansas, Gaye and I have had the joy of observing their beautiful relationship and the way they share their love and their home with others. By consistent example and friendship, by teaching and counsel, they have had a positive effect upon many marriages. Singles of all ages are drawn to them, too. I know of no one more qualified to develop and communicate these concepts for newlyweds and engaged couples. Dan and Gloria, and Gaye and I have a wholehearted commitment to helping others find the wonderful, lasting happiness that God has designed for man and woman in marriage. Our prayer is that this book will come to you in God's timing just as you are making the decision of a lifetime, and that you will find in the clear light of reality the happiness that every couple dreams of.

Your friend in Christ,
Ed Wheat, M.D.

Acknowledgements

Whenever I open a new book, I read the Acknowledgements with keen interest because it helps me to understand the writer in a more personal way.

My "thank you's" are very personal: first, to my beloved family and closest friends, who lived through this time with me, protected me with their prayers, and inspired me with their love.

Also, to my editor, Nia Jones, who knew how to encourage me when I needed it most.

Always, my gratitude to Dr. Wheat. His vision for transformed marriages, his steadfast faith in the Lord Jesus Christ, his love of the Scriptures, his unquenchable hope, and his wisdom and kindness are a continuing inspiration to me. We share one special prayer at every meeting in my office or his: "Lord, please allow us to produce this book to help many couples experience how wonderful a lasting, love-filled marriage can be!"

Gloria Okes Perkins,
Springdale, Arkansas

Introduction

This book has been written for you who are just starting out in marriage because we care about your future. In fact, without knowing you by name, we've been praying for you and picturing you as we have developed this new-marriage handbook.

We asked that our book would find its way into the hands of couples who love each other so much that, in spite of all the statistics, they are determined to build a quality marriage that will last and are seeking to learn how to do it because, realistically, they know it won't be easy. We have the information that you will need to accomplish your goal, along with the solid assurance that, *if you want it badly enough,* a wonderful marriage is within your reach.

We hear from so many people who, not long ago, stood in your place as newlyweds with high expectations of happiness. Now they are wondering what to do about the problems, which have sprung up like fast-growing weeds in what they believed would be their own little Garden of Eden. Most of them acknowledge that they were over-confident: they just assumed their love would carry them through any difficulties. They also say that they were poorly prepared for the realities of marriage. They ask with bewilderment, "Why didn't someone tell us how hard it is to make it work, that it doesn't just happen?" And most of them admit to unrealistic expectations of what marriage would do for them.

Said one young woman, "I thought marriage to my guy would bring automatic happiness with it; I expected it to settle him down and take away all my insecurities. I guess I assumed marriage was some kind of a miracle drug."

Another agreed, "Even though our friends were already getting divorces, we just knew we would be different. We counted on being in love. We thought that would keep us together and make all our dreams come true. But it wasn't enough."

An ex-husband said bitterly, "I wish I'd known some of this sooner. I can look back now and see that our divorce was unnecessary. But we didn't even know enough to know what we didn't know. By the time we tried to get help, it was too late."

Unfortunately, these stories are all too common. Among the disturbing marriage/divorce statistics, here are two that you need to think about. Researchers report that nearly half of all serious marital problems develop in the first two years of marriage. Yet, on the average, couples who seek counseling for the first time have already been married seven years.[1]

Many divorces can be attributed to this five-year counseling gap—a time when the relationship deteriorates, but warning signals are ignored. Usually the couple doesn't seek help until one partner resorts to a drastic move, such as leaving home or having an affair. In our continuing survey over the past five years, it's no wonder that three-fourths of the respondents urge new-marriage counsel as a preventive measure.

We have designed *The First Years of Forever* to stand in this gap by offering you much-needed, but hard-to-obtain, counsel at the time when you need it most, with major chapters devoted to counsel in the critical areas of sex and communication. Next year we will provide a second book to be used as a companion to this one with answers to many of the questions which arise after the first few months of marriage, including financial planning, in-law relationships, decision-making, and strategies for shaping your life together.

We want to include as much as possible to help you build a beautiful marriage. You can participate in the second book by letting us know your needs. We invite you to write us and share your experiences, discoveries, and questions. Send your letter to

Gloria Okes Perkins
The First Years of Forever
P.O. Box 410
Springdale, Arkansas 72764

You have exciting times ahead! As Paul Tournier has said,

> Marriage becomes a great adventure, a continuous discovery both of oneself and of one's mate. It becomes a daily broadening of one's horizon, an opportunity of learning something new about life, about human existence, about God.[2]

If you have not yet married, we encourage you to request a premarriage counseling session with your pastor. In some cases he will use *The First Years of Forever* as a counseling resource; you may even have received your copy as a gift from your church. Remember, as you plan your new life together, that a Bible-believing pastor, and Christian friends can offer tremendous support and encouragement for your marriage.

And now we trust that *The First Years of Forever* will become a well-thumbed "help book" in your home and a good friend during this time of exciting beginnings.

1

The Feelings of Love: Guarding Your Treasure

As newlyweds or an engaged couple, you undoubtedly qualify as experts on the feelings of love. Since few parents today are in the business of arranging marriages, most couples marry because the feelings of love draw them together in an almost irresistible fashion. You know for yourself the euphoric wonder of new love—the magic, the mystery, the miraculous sense of well-being (often described as walking on air) when just being together makes you supremely happy. To love and be loved in this way within the security of marriage is probably one of the greatest pleasures in life.

But can you maintain these wonderful feelings for the next fifty years or more? In our new-marriage handbook, we want to show you how to relate to one another so that you never lose this most precious treasure: your feelings of love.

A dynamic truth that you need to recognize now, at the beginning of your marriage, comes not from a counselor, but a poet. Robert Frost observed that love (like a good poem) *begins in delight and ends in wisdom.*[1] He wasn't saying that delight comes to a dead end because the lovers have learned better. He meant that ecstasy cannot stand still because it has a life of its own. It must move on— hopefully, in the direction of wisdom.

17

What does this say to you? That if you expect your love affair to remain the same or count on it to get better and better without effort on your part, you will be disappointed. Your love relationship must change because it is a living entity. And you will determine the nature of that change by the direction you set now and the course you follow over the years. Your love will either grow or diminish, progress or fall back. It will be more wonderful than you could have imagined, or, for some unhappy couples, it will be dreadful. Some may have to search very hard to find even the faintest trace of love left over from years of neglect.

The feelings of love will always require your attention. Think of it as an investment that yields high returns. Five or seven years down the road your love relationship will reveal just how much both of you have put into it.

LIVING WITH YOUR FEELINGS

To preserve your feelings of love, you need a clear understanding of them—what they are, essentially; what they can and cannot do; and how to nurture and intensify all the good feelings while you confront the negative ones that can threaten your love relationship when you least expect it. Here, in seed form, is the information you need to begin building the love affair of a lifetime. It will happen through treasuring, guarding, and nurturing the feelings of love you now share.

One husband offered this definition of feelings: "Feelings are thoughts of the heart rather than thoughts of the mind." In other words, your feelings give you an inner awareness of your emotional condition from moment to moment.

Your feelings are more immediate than thoughts, of course. They are more like vibrations or signals you must interpret—signs of your humanness. The Lord says in

Psalm 33:15 that He fashions all hearts alike. But some people are more *in touch* with their feelings than others. Individuals differ greatly in their ability to recognize their feelings quickly and interpret them accurately.

Feelings are a gift from God to provide both protection and pleasure. They are indicators that can suggest and offer input, but they have neither authority over you nor power to control you. As children most of us learned we could not always do what we felt like doing. As adults we know that our feelings (our emotions) are not capable of conducting our daily affairs, so we do not give them control. This principle should also apply in our love relationships. Certainly, feelings have helped to bring you together as a newly-married or engaged couple, but they were never designed to *drive* you anywhere.

Your feelings are neither all-powerful nor all-wise. You can appreciate them as indicators—the things that let you know what's happening to you—but never as infallible guides. Only God's Word, the Bible, can guide us surely. If someone tells you, "Do whatever feels good!" BEWARE! Never let your feelings become the deciding factor in anything without checking all the available data first. Respect your feelings, listen to their warnings, but do not let them control you. God has given you a free will and the power to choose. You are in charge.

You must recognize, however, that feelings will always have persuasive force because of their ability to occupy and dominate the moment. George MacDonald describes the deceptive nature of feelings in this way:

> They had a feeling, or a feeling had them, till another feeling came and took its place. When a feeling was there, they felt as if it would never go; when it was gone they felt as if it had never been; when it returned, they felt as if it had never gone.[2]

Feelings are so fragile and explosive that they must be

handled with special care. How you consider your partner's feelings will tell a great deal about you as a lover. As we have already suggested, the feelings of love are the treasure within the earthen vessel of marriage, but they can change unexpectedly, so never look to them as the last word. Always remember, you are *more* than your feelings!

Throughout the Bible God reveals a whole tapestry of feelings. The Song of Solomon offers a vivid display of the feelings of love experienced by a bride and her husband. But nowhere in the New Testament does God ever command us to *feel* anything. Rather, He would have us to behave in certain ways or to adopt certain attitudes, which will produce certain feeling. It is a principle worth learning that if we obey God with right actions, the right feelings will soon follow.

TOUCHING THE MAGIC

Feelings are the music of life and the magic that makes marriage exciting, pleasurable, and satisfying. Let's "touch the magic" by analyzing what happens when a man and woman fall in love. It's important to understand the dynamics of falling in love because they are the very dynamics you will want to keep alive in your marriage relationship. Don't take them for granted because the weight of everyday living can smother the magic of love before you realize it.

Two people falling in love is a powerful emotional event. That it happens to both lovers at the same time intensifies the sense of delight. There is the thrill of newness and a sense of wonder as if the two lovers have entered into a new reality—almost like time-space travel—in which they see themselves and their old world in a different light. C. S. Lewis said, in describing his relationship with his wife Joy, that even his body "had such a different importance" because it was the body his wife loved![3]

The term *falling* accurately depicts the suddenness and drama of the situation. The phrase *in love* correctly implies that the lovers are no longer where they were. They have left themselves as individuals to dwell in a new place together—"a safe and intimate world."

Falling in love has to do with summoning up . . . rapturous feelings of engulfment in a safe and intimate world—one in which two are as one, perfect company, and in which perfect nurturance exists. It has to do with the visions of Eden, buried within, before human aloneness had been perceived.[4]

Four significant things usually occur when love is genuine.

1. The lovers long to be together.

In fact, they may even feel shock-waves of emotion when they must be apart, incomplete when they are separated—a foreshadowing of the time when two will become one in marriage. This powerful sense of need for the other may express itself in a sensation of "home-sickness." This happens because they have become bonded emotionally and now crave that feeling of security and *at-homeness,* which they find only in the other's presence.

As a newlywed told us, "We fell in love one weekend when he came to see me at school. It was incredible! On Thursday I was my own person. On Sunday when I took him to the airport, I was someone new. When he left to board the plane, I thought I would die. . . . I felt so alone, as though half of me had gone with him."

Another bride said, "I used to hate having to say good-by to him. It had nothing to do with wanting to be with him for sexual reasons. I just wanted to be with him! For me, marriage means not having to part at the end of the evening, but being together, whatever we're doing and wherever we happen to be."

2. The lovers see each other in a unique way.

Lovers begin to see each other almost as if through the eyes of God. One husband said, "My wife sees a side of me that no one else sees. I feel as though she knows the true me, and her love filters out all the faults that other people might notice. Maybe this is the way God sees us when our sins have been covered by Jesus Christ. I know that her admiration and acceptance make me want to be my very best."

True romantic love seems to open a lover's eyes to see the loved one the way God sees that person—as extraordinary, priceless, like no one else ever created, as unique with an eternal identity.

The lovers place such high value on each other that they are willing to give up their selfish independence so as to belong to one another. As one young man said, "When I fell in love with her, I knew it meant changing direction for my life. I had planned on a life of travel . . . alone. I valued fast cars and my airplane. But that was worth nothing compared to the value of knowing her and building our life together. Sure, I had a brief, passing regret. But I realized that genuine happiness for me meant loving this girl and being loved by her for the rest of my life. And I haven't been sorry!"

3. The lovers desire to commit themselves to one another.
Real love always wants to commit itself. Judith Adams Perry, M.D., in answering a question about love in a medical magazine, points out that we commit ourselves to whatever we love most:

The *Psychiatric Dictionary* defines love as pleasure. Love usually also involves commitment, regardless of which type of love is expressed—self-love, family, work, spiritual, erotic, or love for life itself. The combination of pleasure and commitment leads to a dynamic process of movement toward the person or ideal.[5]

The Lord Jesus Christ said it first in words we cannot

easily forget: "For where your treasure is, there will your heart be also"(Matt. 6:21).

4. The lovers want to marry, to be together "forever." Falling in love usually leads to the couple's mutual desire to make a new world for themselves, to seal their commitment in marriage. Commitment not only demonstrates the quality of their love but attempts to preserve it . . . forever.

It seems there is an intrinsic connection between "forever" and some commitments. The most convincing way that people have hit upon to state the fact that they are not placing conditions on the giving of themselves to another is to confess that they are not setting a predetermined time span within which the relationship is to work. In other words, the most congenial way we humans have of showing that our commitments are unconditional is to say "forever." Granted this is a resort to quantity terms in order to prove quality, but who has found a better way to express total commitment to another person than to say that we include him or her in our entire future? . . . Commitment is the most natural way of . . . expressing the love one has for another . . . and of proving as well as preserving that same love. All other things being equal, permanence will be a property of every commitment that flows from love and continues in love.[6]

If all these exciting events have occurred, can we then conclude that they will "live happily ever after"? No. We don't know if they will apply wisdom in their relationship as they shape their lives together. But this is the place where most couples begin—this period of falling in love. And the principles involved in falling in love can help any couple stay in love and grow in love. Here they are in capsule form:

STAYING IN LOVE

1. Concentrate on building an intimate relationship. Nurture each other emotionally. Touch lovingly, share thoughts and feelings. Spend private time together so that you can continue to feel secure and at home in each other's presence.

2. Avoid the negatives that could change the way you see each other. Live in an atmosphere of approval, and forgive quickly and generously.

3. Live out your commitment to one another in such a way that strong links of trust are established and maintained. Build your marriage on a solid biblical base.

4. Build your marriage on a solid biblical base. Always think and talk in "forever" terms.

Now let us share with you one of the fascinating surprises of marriage. If—and this is an important *if*—you both move from the falling-in-love stage to the in-love stage and, even more importantly, into the practice of *loving* your partner (which involves giving and always doing the very best for him or her), you will have the delightful experience of falling in love all over again many times during the course of a full and happy marriage. All the enjoyable emotions will be there, even the sense of fresh wonder, of seeing each other and life itself through love-washed eyes.

BEWARE OF THE MYTH

We have analyzed the experience of falling in love; now let's examine the widely held myth that falling in love is an uncontrollable event.

As an illustration imagine being married, but things are not going well in your relationship. You feel distant from your mate, maybe offended. You begin having intimate talks at work with someone who is lonely and sympathetic. Your eyes meet across the room; you begin sharing secrets; your hands touch, and presto! the magic strikes and you think you're in love. Your emotions have you convinced that, obviously, you don't love your mate anymore. "It's no one's fault," you say. "It just happened."

Wrong!!! Your feelings, which can get out of "sync" temporarily, are playing tricks on you, and you are experiencing the impulses of an infatuation that you incorrectly label "love," although it has very little in common with what genuine love is or how it behaves.

This, of course, has been an exercise in imagination. But one young man who came in for counseling—we'll call him Jim—had just such an experience. His wife Beth was working the night shift as a nurse to make extra money to furnish their new home. Jim didn't see much of her, and when he did, they were usually both tired and frustrated. Then Jim became acquainted with a co-worker who was going through the trauma of divorce. Sympathy drew him to her at first, but soon he was infatuated and thrilled by this woman's dependence on him. Jim was also bewildered. How could he love two women at once? Should he move out of his home? Should he seek a divorce? He suddenly felt obligated to both women, and sought counsel.

Jim's feelings were playing tricks on him. He had only one commitment —the one he had made four years ago when he married Beth. What he was experiencing had no real control over him, regardless of how powerful his emotions were toward this woman. To save his marriage, Jim needed to stop spending time with this woman, to ignore the feelings, and rearrange his life so he and his wife could have time together to fall in love all over again.

Beth was able to change her work schedule, and she and Jim began pouring their lives into loving each other. Jim recognized his deceptive feelings for what they were, and the co-worker turned her sights elsewhere. The episode ended happily for Jim and Beth.

The message of this true story—which is played out in ten thousand cities around the country—is that the feelings of love cannot survive alone. They must be accompanied by the facts of love. Then "walking on air" becomes moving ahead together on solid ground, and delight is transformed by wisdom into something even better.

The ABCs of Forever: Living by the Facts of Love

The title of our book, *The First Years of Forever,* carries with it a promise—that we will show you how to form a forever relationship with the one you love. But what is a forever relationship? You will find the "ABCs" of it in this chapter.

Let's start by thinking of a forever relationship as the kind that begins with the best intentions. A man says to his fiancee, "Sweetheart, I want to be with you *forever.*" And she whispers, "I'm yours for the rest of our lives—and *forever!*" Five years later he's lost his job, they've quit communicating, and their sex life is almost nonexistent. What happened to "forever?" As one young man said, sadly, "It's like a dream we lost along the way."

The forever relationship does not have to be a dream that vanishes in the light of cold, hard day. In fact, it will actually thrive on adversity and become more precious when the rest of life has temporarily lost its joy. How does one acquire anything so valuable? Well, it cannot be found or fallen into, but *formed*—by a man and a woman who want it enough to pour their lives into the building process.

First, it must be understood. So let's consider the fundamentals—the ABCs of forever.

Most couples begin with love. But who can say how love really begins? Each of you has a different story to tell, for romantic love takes surprising turns in its development. For one person, love warms slowly out of a good friendship; for another, love sparks a blaze fueled by sexual desire. Love may begin with admiration in the classroom, or find its root in good conversation on a blind date. Perhaps you discovered someone who really understands you, and life seems magically transformed because you are no longer alone! It matters little whether your love found its beginning when you first locked eyes with someone across a crowded room, or whether you've been in love since you met in junior high. If it leads to your passionate desire to belong to each other exclusively, you are embarking on the adventure of a lifetime.

BELONGING LOVE

We can call this kind of love that first sparks a relationship *belonging* love and let it represent all that is delightful and exciting and comforting about loving and being loved.

As Malachi Martin has described it,

> The surest effect of love in an individual is an increase of what we all recognize as happiness. It is unmistakable. When we love, and are loved, that happiness is irrepressible in us. Like fresh spring water, it bathes everything within us and spills out into our lives. It seeks to splash and sparkle and wash the world about us until everything in and around us reflects a new light.[1]

As wonderful as belonging love is, it cannot be counted on to produce the forever relationship lovers long for. *Belonging love,* though it seems perfect for the moment, is not guaranteed to last, even within the context of a marriage. The Bible compares this kind of love, which can change so quickly, to the dew of early morning and the misty clouds that disappear before the day is half begun (Hos. 6:4). And our country's rising divorce rate suggests that the institution of marriage has seemingly lost its power to bond a couple together in a lasting relationship.

THE MISSING ELEMENTS

What is missing if the best love two people can have for each other in marriage cannot be depended upon? The story of a couple we'll call Joe and Evie best illustrates the problem of missing elements in a relationship.

When they married in their late teens, Joe and Evie displayed all the signs of two people in love. "She was the most beautiful girl I had ever seen," Joe said. "We're in our forties now, and she's still a very lovely woman. We've gone through tough times together financially and survived. We've gone through grief and trouble. We lost our oldest son in an automobile accident when he was sixteen, and our youngest daughter has had a bad marriage and emotional problems. But she's doing okay. Evie and I could really begin to enjoy life now if only . . ."

Joe's "if only" meant, if only Evie had not filed for divorce. Her reason for wanting to end the marriage went back many years to their newlywed experiences. Their sexual relationship had been less than fulfilling for Evie, but the couple had never sought help for their problem. Instead, she became increasingly resentful and avoided sex. This continued until Joe's mother died unexpectedly.

"Then I was desperate for comfort and love," Joe said. "I turned to my wife, but when she was so cold and kept rejecting me, I found someone else. I ran around for close to two years, although Evie and I had a son during this time. It was seeing myself as a father that caused me to straighten up and get my act together. I asked Evie to forgive me, and I promised to be a good husband and father. I've never been unfaithful to her since. I've tried to make it up to her."

Unfortunately, things continued to go badly for this

couple. As Joe tells it, "She never forgave me, I guess. Held a grudge against me all this time. She even told me recently that she blamed me for our son's death. Said it wouldn't have happened if we hadn't moved to this part of the country. She's just been waiting, evidently, until the financial conditions were right for us to divorce.

"But," he went on, "I thought we had a good life together. I still love her although she says she has no love for me, that I killed it when I went out with other women so many years ago. So we're dividing our property, our kids are divided over the situation, and we're both facing middle age alone with nothing to look forward to. I can't believe it turned out like this. We were so much in love when we married!"

So much in love when they were married . . . Such is the refrain of many failed marriages. But Joe and Evie, like others, lacked the love that never fails, the love that could have given them a compassionate tenderness for one another and a longing to meet one another's needs; the love that heals all bitterness and makes forgiveness possible. Married, yes. But they lacked the essential ingredient of *commitment* to their marriage covenant and to each other.

A *LOVE-CENTERED* MARRIAGE

To form a forever relationship, you will need a *Love-centered* marriage. The love you have at the beginning with its intensely personal quality of belonging and possessing fluctuates because it is fed by feelings, and feelings change, especially if needs and desires are not being met. But the God of Love has made His own love available to each of us. That love, which the Bible calls *agape,* never changes. It is unconditional and does not depend on a person's behavior. It goes right on showing kindness to the beloved, no matter what, because it is controlled not by our emotions, but by our will. The ability to love this way is a

30

gift from God through His Son Jesus Christ; His love channeled through us blesses our mate and our marriage. The nature of agape love is described in our book, *LOVE LIFE for Every Married Couple*:

> Out of His own mighty nature, God supplies the resources for this love, and they are available to any life connected with His by faith in Jesus Christ: "God's love has been poured out in our hearts through the Holy Spirit Who has been given to us" (Rom. 5:5 THE AMPLIFIED BIBLE). This is the agape love of the New Testament—unconditional, unchanging, inexhaustible, generous beyond measure, and most wonderfully kind![2]

ABSOLUTE LOVE

It is important for you to understand that the love you feel for each other needs to be grounded in agape love. This love is *Absolute* love and comes directly from God; there is no substitute for it, and you could never crank it out on your own. Consider some of the synonyms for the word "absolute" to help you better understand the nature of this love: actual, authentic, bona fide, genuine, indisputable, real, sure, true, undeniable, complete, consummate (which means perfect), and godlike.

We have, then, two loves that merge into one to bless our life together: *absolute* love and *belonging* love. Both need to be at the heart of a relationship. These loves can only be fully enjoyed within the protective structure God has designed. We might think of the structure of marriage as our House of Love. We enter this house by our free choice. Our decision is both legal and public, and, most importantly, spiritual. When we marry we cannot escape the fact (even if we wanted to) that we are entering into a sacred covenant, established and ordained by God from the beginning of human history. As Jay Adams has said in his book *Marriage, Divorce and Remarriage* :

God designed marriage as the foundational element of all human society. Before there was . . . a church, a school, a business instituted, God formally instituted marriage, declaring, "A man shall leave his father and mother and shall cleave to his wife, and the two shall become one flesh."

Dr. Adams also points out that

if marriage were of human origin, then human beings would have a right to set it aside. But since God instituted marriage, only He has the right to do so. . . . Nor can marriage be regulated according to human whims. [It] is subject to the rules and regulations set down by God. If He had said nothing more about marriage after establishing it, we might have proceeded to draw up such rules on our own. But He did not leave us in the dark; God has revealed His will about marriage in the pages of the Bible.[3]

COMMITMENT TO MARRIAGE

But one of our problems is that marriage today is taken so lightly. It is no longer a place of safety. Only through *commitment* to the absolute permanence of marriage, a commitment made by both partners, based on deep beliefs and the choice of the will, can marriage become the sure guardian of love. If we have made this once-and-for-all-time commitment, the structure of marriage will preserve our love. And the couple who has undergirded their marriage by their commitment will be prepared for those inevitable times when their marriage will be tested.

Those who have given up on a love-filled, enduring marriage do not understand the ABCs of forever: *Absolute* love strengthens and turns to pure gold our *Belonging* love, and *Commitment* to the permanence of marriage guards and preserves our love relationship for the rest of our lives.

A *FOREVER* RELATIONSHIP

To answer the question posed earlier in this chapter: A forever relationship consists of a Love-centered life built and shared by a man and a woman who maintain total commitment to one another and to their marriage as the permanent structure of their lives on this earth, and as the safeguard of their love—a love which has its origin and continuance in the eternal love of God and thus never ends.

The biblical equation for a forever relationship is this:

> Absolute Love +
> Belonging Love +
> Commitment to Marriage =
> a Forever Relationship

HEAVEN'S RESOURCES

During premarriage counseling sessions we ask the engaged couple, "How do you plan to celebrate your twenty-fifth wedding anniversary?" While this may seem to be the least of their concerns, the question is more relevant than they know. The marriage that lasts and lasts happily begins with the confident assurance that there will be a twenty-fifth wedding anniversary, or a fiftieth or more if God permits.

We'd like to give you some good reasons for this assurance, even in a day when divorce *seems* to be a natural consequence of marriage. We call these Heaven's Resources. They are truths you can count upon concerning God's readiness to help you build the kind of marriage you dream of now.

1. It is God's will in every marriage that the couple love each other with an absorbing spiritual, emotional, and physical attraction that continues to grow throughout their lifetime together.

God intends for you and your mate to experience this love-bond together, not with substitutes, and will show you how to bring this about.

2. Because God is the one who made you, who thought up the idea of marriage and ordained it for your blessing and

gives you the capacity to love, He is the one who knows best how to build love into your particular relationship. You can trust Him to be intimately involved in your efforts to develop a love-filled marriage.

A third principle follows logically from these great truths:

3. It is possible for any Christian couple to develop this love relationship in their marriage because it is in harmony with God's express will.

If the time should come when you are feeling discouraged about your relationship, remember that Heaven's Resources are at your disposal. Any couple who want and choose to build a love-filled marriage *can* do so.

To sum up the counsel of these first two chapters, here is a sure formula for a lasting, love-filled marriage: Enjoy the *feelings* of love and guard them well, but live by the *facts* of love.

Keep the delights of your love
ever-green and growing
by planting their roots deep into truth
and watering them with wisdom.

3

Faithfulness:
The First Essential

How would you answer this question: What one quality do you believe will contribute most to the continuing development of love and growth in your marriage relationship?

Think about it! Finding the most satisfactory answer to this question will give you insight into what will be most important in building your forever relationship.

This question was recently put to a husband and wife who have loved each other for more than a quarter century. Their responses were completely honest since each gave a response without knowing how the other responded. Consider their answers. What essentials have been at work to make their marriage last?

The wife took her time before giving an answer, obviously considering the many good aspects of their relationship. "It has to be *faithfulness,*" she finally said. "Steve's faithfulness to me all these years is so unmistakable that I don't have to live with fear and uncertainty. I never doubt that he will *be there,* loving me as long as he has strength left in his body."

She also added, "The two qualities that mean almost as much as faithfulness are Steve's tremendous *kindness*—I can always count on him to be kind!—and his *responsiveness* to me. I never go to him for comfort that his arms do

35

not open to receive me. And if I reach out, his hand is always there, warm and strong and waiting for me.

"But as I thought about it," she went on, "I realized that his kindness and responsiveness are just other ways of showing his faithfulness to me!"

Steve answered the same question with a prompt assurance. "Whatever you want to call it," he said, "the most important quality is being able to trust my wife. I trust her to be true to me, and I trust her to keep on loving me, looking out after my best interests, and being loyal to me. That's the bottom line."

What is particularly interesting about this couple's answers is that in designing this new-marriage handbook, we reached similar conclusions about those qualities that make for a lasting marriage.

How then can you make faithfulness, this first essential quality, a cornerstone of your relationship?

Faithfulness in marriage means firmly adhering to the commitment you have made. In both attitude and action you are loyal, true, and constant to your marriage partner. Although *faithfulness* implies *duty,* with an allegiance, vows, and promises to live up to, the husband and wife who are truly faithful live out their loyalty to one another not out of duty, but joy.

This loving loyalty has two requirements. First, a faithful couple must never allow a third person to intrude into their love relationship. When you are faithful to your mate, you not only avoid adultery, you don't even give the appearance of interest in another person. Your partner should never feel the need to compete with someone else for your attention or admiration.

The second requirement for faithfulness involves loving your partner in ways that meet his or her needs and deepest desires. We can never plead ignorance as to how to do this; in the Scriptures God has shown us how to faithfully love one another. (See chapters 8 and 9.)

Faithfulness begins as a choice. It is, in fact, always a choice. As one Christian therapist has explained:

> Central to marriage is this "choosing" process wherein a unique relationship with one person is established. What keeps it vital is a faithfulness which continues to choose the same person even in the midst of pain, frustration and disillusionment. Apart from this, the institution of marriage cannot sustain the blush of its initial days or the vows of its partners.[1]

The ongoing choice to be faithful to the one you have chosen makes all the difference between an empty relationship (in which one or both eventually look for other ways to meet their emotional needs) and a warm, vital, intimate relationship, which continues to grow in the security of steadfast love.

Faithfulness is not only an ongoing choice. It is a continuing call to action. If you don't express it, if you don't demonstrate it in your daily life, it can't be faithfulness.

To illustrate faithfulness at work, consider this true story told in *What Will Make My Marriage Work?* A couple was married only a year when the wife became ill with multiple sclerosis. Unable to bear the thought of being a burden to her husband, this young woman decided she would "set him free." But her husband refused to leave her. Instead he showered tender care and love on her as long as she lived. Why did he do it? "Because," he said, "when I vowed before God 'for better or for worse' and 'in sickness and in health,' I meant it." Did he ever regret it? No! This faithful husband emphatically remarked, "God made both of us unbelievably happy."[2]

By contrast, consider another true story of a husband whose wife of many years came to the last months of her terminal illness. He decided that he could not give her all the attention she needed, because it was necessary for his survival to live his own life, which must come first.

Both men had made their vows, but only one continued to choose faithfulness under difficult circumstances. One man lived his faithfulness; the other, his own life. Their actions reflected their choices.

While few of you will be forced to make such difficult choices early in your marriage, later in life one mate may need tender, protective care because of serious health problems. There is great comfort when you can count on each other to be faithful, whatever comes. This sense of security cannot depend on blind faith. You may have gone into marriage with blind faith, but now you must build trust and faithfulness. The ways you demonstrate your faithfulness today will build bridges of trust for a lifetime. Here are seven ways to demonstrate faithfulness.

1. Behave in faithful ways consistently. As the Bible says, "Ever follow that which is good"(1 Thess. 5:15).

In other words, do everything you can to express your faithfulness in action. Support and encourage your partner by helping out whenever and wherever it is possible. When you see a job that needs to be done, do it without being asked. Be consistently honest in all your dealings, showing yourself trustworthy in even the smallest detail. As a troubled wife once said, "It takes a lot of energy to love someone you can't trust!" Being trustworthy means keeping your word. If you say you will meet your mate at a certain place and time, make sure you are there. Most of all, show kindness in your actions, not just your words. You've heard the old expression, "Pretty is as pretty does." Well, love *is* as love *does*.

2. Avoid doing things to offend or disappoint your mate, and don't do anything to create suspicion in your partner's mind. As the Bible says, "Abstain from all appearance of evil"(1 Thess. 5:22).

Consider these two cases of couples who received

counseling because of problems in their marriage. The husband had a habit of casually putting his arm around other women in social situations. It meant nothing to him, but it disturbed his wife, and consequently affected their relationship. In another case, the wife sometimes praised other men she admired and respected. Her husband felt threatened, believing his wife found him inadequate compared to other men. If you are unsure whether some action may offend your mate, ask yourself this: "Will this seem like faithfulness or unfaithfulness to my mate?"

3. Let your partner know that being faithful brings you joy; you are not faithful just out of a sense of duty. Be happy and show it! As the Bible says, "Rejoice evermore" (1 Thess. 5:16).

Your happiness is the greatest compliment you can give your loved one, and the expression of joy gives marriage vitality. But sometimes one partner will go through times of sadness, brooding, worry, or depression. And the other will also experience some anguish, wondering: "Have I done something wrong? Doesn't my mate love me anymore? If my partner's not happy, it must be my fault." Be open with each other during these times, reassure each other, and pray together about all your concerns.

4. Consistently show appreciation for all the ways your partner blesses your life. Thank him or her for even the smallest things. Speak positively about your partner to other people, and give thanks to God, too. As the Bible says, "In everything give thanks. . ." (1 Thess. 5:18).

Showing appreciation not only demonstrates faithfulness to your partner, it builds more loving faithfulness in your own heart. It is amazing how we tend to believe our own spoken words. So be careful what you say and always speak positively.

5. Learn to be sensitive to your partner in even the smallest detail. A faithful lover goes to a great deal of trouble

to understand the beloved. Quench not the spirit of your mate through misunderstandings!

Take the case of Karen and Gary. Karen's family had always made much of birthdays, while Gary could forget his own birthday if not reminded. When Gary casually postponed his wife's birthday celebration to the weekend when it would be a more convenient time, Karen felt devastated and unloved. Gary had made some special plans for her he thought would delight her, so he was astonished when Karen was hostile and tearful that day. "But why didn't you give me my birthday card on my birthday anyway?" she exclaimed. "That would have made it all right." Gary could only answer, "Because I didn't think. Because I didn't know the timing was so important to you." It's up to you to *know* what's important to your mate.

Keep in mind how different you and your partner are— not just your backgrounds, but your emotional make-up. You cannot demonstrate faithfulness if you do not "dwell together according to knowledge" (1 Peter 3:7). Learn what really matters to your partner, learn his or her emotional language of love, and then act accordingly.

6. Pray that you will be faithful. It's not always easy to be what your partner needs, and we can use all the help we can get. The Bible says, "Pray without ceasing" (1 Thess. 5:17). Keep the goal of faithfulness ever uppermost in your mind, and maintain a heart attitude of prayer.

Praying will keep you alert and watchful of anything that might draw you away from the oneness of the marriage relationship. If a passing fantasy about some other attractive person has you distracted, a prayerful attitude will redirect your focus. Pray for faithfulness in every season of life.

7. Look to God who is the faithful One. What you can't do in your own strength, He can empower you to do. The Scripture says, "Faithful is he that calleth you who also will do it"(1 Thess. 5:24).

Forgiveness:
The Second Essential

Marriage becomes a series of surprises for most of us, and one of them is how frequently we need to forgive and be forgiven. Faithfulness may be the first essential of a love-filled marriage, but even the best relationship cannot remain intact for long without forgiveness: the second essential of marriage.

EVERY MARRIAGE NEEDS THE HEALING TOUCH

Every husband-and-wife combination needs the healing touch of forgiveness. Where else could there be more opportunity to annoy, insult, offend, or ruffle another person than in the intimacy of married life when we're constantly under foot, get in each other's way, and have to share all things in common (whether we like it or not)? That's just ordinary living, without taking into account the astonishingly hurtful things husbands and wives do, which demand more forgiveness than any of us could work up on our own.

To learn how to forgive, and how to draw on spiritual resources to accomplish the task, is one of the most important "skills" newlyweds can acquire. *Skill* seems an inadequate word for something as glorious as forgiveness, but it's a beginning point.

FORGIVENESS AS A WAY OF LIFE

Think, for a moment, of forgiveness as a way of life. Picture your relationship growing year by year with forgiveness as an essential nutrient in the soil of your marriage, keeping your love alive and thriving. Or think of forgiveness as an element of the emotional air you breathe, as important as oxygen in the physical world; a natural ingredient in the wholesome environment of your marriage. In other words, forgiveness needs to become habitual in your relationship—something both of you do lovingly, consistently, and *forgetfully* because you don't keep score!

What is forgiveness? There's some confusion about that. When most people think of forgiveness, they think of changing their feeling toward someone who has wronged them, of teary-eyed sweetness replacing anger and a thirst for revenge.

But forgiveness is not a feeling at all. It is a choice you make, which may go against every self-centered fiber of your being. So forget the easy, mushy sentiment that the world inserts into the idea. True, you may feel some emotions when you forgive, perhaps gladness at being reconciled and close again. But if you are acting only on sentimental impulse, there's no assurance that your forgiveness will last beyond that impulsive moment. True forgiveness is a strong, rational decision based on spiritual values, fueled by spiritual resources, and modeled after the spiritual principle of God's forgiveness.

HOW GOD'S FORGIVENESS WORKS

To understand how forgiveness can work in your marriage relationship, it's necessary to go to the Bible to understand the quality of God's forgiveness. Although the entire New Testament resonates with the wonder of God's forgiveness through Jesus Christ, one verse will suffice for our purpose "And be kind to one another, tender-hearted, forgiving each other, just as God in Christ also has forgiven you" (Ephes. 4:32 NASV).

1, Be kind, *chrestoi* (what is fitting to a need).

2. Be compassionate, *eusplanchnoi* (tender-hearted).

3. Be forgiving,*charizomenoi* (giving freely and graciously as a favor).

4. Just as God in Christ has forgiven (another form of the same verb, *charizomai*) you.

The same wonderful word is used here for forgiveness whether it be divine or human. *Charizomai* means to bestow a favor graciously, unconditionally, and freely. It represents a gracious, beautiful act of showing favor—the favor, grace, and goodness of God to man—of the worthy to the unworthy.

Obviously, we can't forgive like this on our own, but if we have experienced this favor ourselves—God's personal forgiveness through Jesus Christ—then we can draw upon this resource in our marriage. When husband and wife are both in Christ—both pouring out this gracious, beautiful favor upon one another—what a love-filled marriage they can have!

This much is clear then. We can forgive because we have been forgiven first. We can learn how to forgive from God's example. And we can draw upon His resources to show this gracious favor to one another.

FORGIVENESS IS A PROMISE

The next question is, how do we show this gracious favor? Jay Adams explains in *More Than Redemption,*

Forgiveness is a *promise*. When God forgives a sinner, He does not simply become emotional over his repentance. No, instead, He goes on record that He has forgiven by making (and keeping) a promise to that effect: "Your sins and iniquities will I remember against you no more. . . ." (Jer. 31:34).

Our forgiveness is modeled after God's forgiveness (Ephes. 4:32). That means that for us forgiveness is also a promise that offers assurance for the future. So when a counselee says, "I forgive you," to another, then he also makes a promise. This . . . is an essential element of forgiveness.[1]

Dr. Adams defines forgiveness as

a formal declaration to lift the burden of one's guilt and a promise to remember another's wrong against him no more.

HOW FORGIVENESS WORKS IN A CRISIS

Let's test this definition by writing a scenario to use as an example. A husband (we'll call him Mark) has deeply wounded his wife (we'll call her Lucinda) by paying too much attention to her former college roommate (Shirley) at a party. They have a stormy discussion after they get home. (She's sending forth the thunder bolts; he's trying to come in out of the rain.) He finally manages to communicate that he feels bad about it, that it meant nothing, and he wishes she could forgive him.

Lucinda would prefer to stay angry; after all, he deserves it! But she remembers three things: how much she loves him; how important forgiveness is in a marriage; and how Christ forgave her when she had done many things worse than this. So she makes the choice to forgive him. They pray together, agree on the way they both should behave at parties in the future, and they go to sleep in each other's arms.

Much More Than an Emotional Episode

This is much more than an emotional episode. By her choice to forgive, Lucinda has made a promise to Mark, just as God made a promise to His people. She has lifted the burden of guilt from him; he doesn't have to get up tomorrow morning shamefaced, trying to stay on her good side. He doesn't carry the burden anymore.

But there's more to the promise than that. God's forgiveness involves never remembering the sin against his people again. Lucinda's promise also includes a three-part commitment, whether stated or not: "I won't bring this up to you again, Mark. I won't bring it up to others either. I won't tell my sister or my best girlfriend, and I won't make a scene with Shirley." And, now comes the hard part, the third part. She also promises, "I won't bring this up to myself again. I will remember it no more!"

Feelings Have Nothing to Do With It

(Note: Lucinda did not feel like making the promise. Not really. She was steamed! How dare he sit and talk to Shirley all evening! But she made the conscious decision to forgive.)

The next morning while she's scrambling eggs, the anger begins slowly building again. Now she has to make the choice to keep her promise whether or not she feels like it. So she asks God to help her show love to Mark, and she greets Mark with a kiss. After breakfast, they have their Bible reading together, and she surprises him by helping him wash the car. (She even vacuums the interior, the part he doesn't like to do.)

When Self-Pity Returns. . . .

By this time, she *feels* warm and loving and they have a wonderful weekend together. All goes well until she's sitting in the dentist's office three days later. Something (she doesn't know what) triggers her memory of that party, and the awful way she felt, and *how could Mark do that to me?!?* Suddenly, she's full of self-pity and in danger, once again, of breaking her promise.

But Lucinda understands how to handle such situations. She does not allow her thoughts to run wild, and she doesn't argue with them. Instead, she looks away from them and occupies her mind in another way. Pulling out her purse organizer, she begins making a menu list for their camping trip in the mountains. The moment passes, and God does His part. In fact, she forgets the emotional pain of the event so completely that when she runs into Shirley at the mall two months later, she can give her an untroubled smile and a friendly greeting. Later, the happening itself fades from her memory, and if remembered at all, she does not relive it. It is like something that occurred long ago and far away. She has forgiven biblically, and God has enabled her to forget.

A Good Pattern Established

Mark learns several lessons, too: (1) that he was a jerk, who needs to give more thought to his wife's feelings, (He confesses his sin to God and asks God to make him more sensitive to her needs.); (2) that his wife is a beautiful person, and not in looks only, (He has more respect and thankfulness for her.); and (3) that the next time she offends him (which does happen occasionally) he'll be quick to forgive her in turn. Lucinda's choice to forgive has established the beginning of a blessed pattern in their marriage.

THE FOUR STEPS OF FORGIVENESS

Here, in review, are the four steps of forgiveness:

1. Choose, with your free will, to forgive.

2. Make the promise to lift the burden of guilt from the person as far as the wrong against you is concerned. Remember the person's sin no more—never naming it again to the person, to others, or to yourself.

3. Seal it with your behavior, demonstrating love in suitable ways with tender-hearted kindness, and doing what the Bible shows you to be right in the situation.

47

4. Trust God to allow you to forget and to renew your mind with new attitudes.

WHEN YOU WON'T FORGIVE

What if you choose not to forgive? What if you prefer to hold on to the resentments, the anger, the hurt? God's Word makes the consequences of this choice plain. So, let's look at the options.

1. If you hold on to your resentments, they will turn to bitterness. As a result, your life will be poisoned, and others' lives, too.

"Be careful that none of you fails to respond to the grace of God, for if he does there can spring up in him a bitter spirit which can poison the lives of many others" (Heb. 12:15 PHILLIPS).

2. By refusing to release the burden of the other person's wrong against you and choosing to carry that burden yourself, you may become crippled in the living of life. God warns us about spiritual lameness,

Make straight paths for your feet, lest that which is lame be turned out of the way; but let it rather be healed. Follow peace with all men, and holiness, without which no man shall see the Lord; looking diligently lest any man fail of the grace of God, lest any root of bitterness springing up trouble you, and by it many be defiled (Heb. 12:13–15).

3. If you are not willing to forgive, there is no way you can expect to walk in personal fellowship with God. A Christian's forgiveness is based on realizing he has been forgiven, as we read in Ephesians 4:32. Choosing to withhold this forgiveness from others will erect a barrier between you and your God.

For if ye forgive men their trespasses, your heavenly Father will also forgive you; But if ye forgive not men their trespasses, neither will your Father forgive your trespasses (Matt. 6:14–15).

David Augsburger in *The Freedom of Forgiveness* challenges his readers to learn the power of love to overcome every bitterness of the heart. But to those who would reject the freedom of forgiveness he warns,

> If you intend to claim all your rights in life, to even all scores against you, to demand every penny ever owed to you, then go ahead.
>
> But if you give no inch, expect no second chances; if you show no mercy, do not hope for mercy; if you extend no forgiveness you can expect none. Life, love, mercy and forgiveness are all two-way streets. To receive, you must give. Humbly. Aware that you are constantly in need of the understanding and acceptance of others and the loving mercy of God.[2]

Granted, the scenario we used as an example was not a pivotal moment in life. It was an easy wrong to forgive compared to those we hear about every day from heart-broken and embittered husbands and wives. We trust nothing like that has occurred in your new marriage. But it is good to learn the principles of forgiveness so thoroughly that if the worst should happen, you will be prepared to handle it in God's way. We can assure you that far more suffering results from unforgiveness and its continuing effects than from the original injury.

A CLEAR CHOICE

It's really simple, after all. You either choose love and emotional freedom and fullness of life, or you hold on to old injuries and let them grow inside of you until they take over and you become their prisoner. You are not hurting the one who sinned against you. All the damage you would like to inflict on that one comes back on you instead. It's a principle of life. It's the law of sowing and reaping: "Be not deceived, God is not mocked, for whatever a man soweth, that shall he also reap" (Gal. 6:7).

Love cannot grow in the same heart with negative attitudes and bad feelings—anger, bitterness, resentment, pride, despair, or hostility (veiled or otherwise). So always be careful what you are growing in your marriage.

WHEN IT SEEMS IMPOSSIBLE TO FORGIVE

If you are ever faced with the need to forgive and you feel it's impossible, remember these things:

1. God never asks His children to do anything that He does not provide both the instructions for and the strength to accomplish. You have the instructions in this chapter, and He will give you the strength if you call on Him for it, and then do what is right.

2. You do not have to be controlled by your feelings, and you are not the helpless prisoner of your past. People sometimes picture themselves as enslaved by their own feelings, as prisoners of events that happened in the past. And yet Christians have already been set free. Jesus said,

You will know the truth, and the truth will set you free. . . . If the Son sets you free, you will be free indeed (John 8:32, 36 NIV).

If you are a Christian, trusting in Jesus Christ alone for your salvation, right now you are *free*. If you believe it and act on it, you will experience the truth of it.

3. Jesus Christ has special deliverance and healing for you if you have been bruised and wounded by the sins of your mate—or anyone else—against you. Recall the words He used to describe His ministry.

The Spirit of the Lord is upon me, because he hath anointed me to . . . set at liberty them that are bruised (Luke 4:18).

As we explained in *LOVE LIFE,*

There is no bruise, no emotional wound in your marriage that the Lord cannot heal when you choose to forgive and commit this matter and your subsequent behavior to Him. No hatred can hold you prisoner when you choose freedom. No negative attitude can dominate you when you choose to let it go as an act of obedience to the Lord Jesus Christ. His love simply overpowers old resentments. It is like raising the shade and opening the window in that dark room. The sunshine floods in and dispels every corner of darkness. The air is fresh and sweet and exhilarating.[3]

DO WE HAVE TO FORGIVE EVERYTHING?

Is there any sin that you can't be expected to forgive? Sometimes people tell us, "I can forgive everything but *that*." The answer is that God is not selective with us. When He forgives us in Christ, He forgives everything. So please remember that God's grace, (from which comes *charizomai* in Ephes. 4:32) covers *every category of wrongdoing*.

Dr. Wheat's personal philosophy has always been "Anger against someone is a big waste of time. It doesn't bother the other person, but it drains your own energy. You're the loser." He says, "If someone is hostile toward me, it's their problem, not mine. As for forgiveness, I don't argue with God about it. I just do it. And I sleep well at night."

As a couple in love, planning a forever relationship, you need to get your forgiveness skills in good working order: you will have plenty of practice on the small things. We pray the larger things never put you to the test. But if they do, you can forgive in the biblical way we have outlined here. Hold to His way of handling the situation, and God will take care of the "forgetting" part for you.

FORGIVENESS IN YOUR LOVE RELATIONSHIP

Here's how forgiveness can take its place in your love relationship, soothing the irritations and healing the hurts, which occur even between two people who love each other very much, and, afterward, restoring your sense of oneness.

1. Make a habit of forgiving and never keep count.

2. Settle your accounts quickly. It's best to forgive one another before you go to sleep. Some couples commit themselves to kissing and saying "I love you" before they go to sleep at night. If they can't do that, they work on the conflict until it is resolved. Then they go to sleep. We encourage you to never, even for one night, withhold your love, mercy, and compassion from your partner.

3. Remember that forgiveness always includes the idea of restoration and a new start. Maintain that sense of newness in your relationship. Whenever you have resolved a problem and given each other the gracious favor of forgiveness, you can enjoy a fresh beginning in your marriage. Then, as the poet says, you "wake at dawn with winged heart and give thanks for another day of loving."

When we forgive habitually, quickly, and expectantly, we can look forward to the continuing inflow of His mercies in our marriage—"new every morning."

5

Communicating:
Your Lifeline in Marriage

Communication is one of the extraordinary delights of marriage, when it's working. *Nothing,* not even sexual fulfillment, will bring as much enriching intimacy into your relationship.

But it's more than a luxurious pleasure. Call it the *lifeline* of a love-filled marriage—the means by which indispensable supplies are transported from husband to wife, and from wife to husband.

LIFELINE SUPPLIES

If you have good communication in your marriage, the lifeline will provide these supplies:

- **The knowledge and understanding of one another which you need for intimate closeness**

- **The interchange of information and ideas you need to work together as a husband-wife team**

- **The capability to work out your differences and resolve your conflicts**

- **The continuing "in touch" contact you must have to grow together in the same direction, and to be there to support each other during the changes and difficult times of life.**

Obviously, couples trying to operate without these

supplies will encounter major problems. In the troubled marriages we counsel, communication lines are almost always clogged or severed. In fact, researchers believe that 90 percent of all marriage counseling involves the attempt to restore communication, or to teach the couple to communicate effectively for the very first time.

It's easy when you're dating and lulled by soft lights and romance to assume that you communicate well, but under the floodlight of marriage, any flaws or trouble spots in your communication system will quickly show up. Domeena C. Renshaw, M.D., an expert on communication in marriage, explains: "Soon after marriage, as daily routines evolve, there is less talk but many more (frequently inaccurate) assumptions about what the other thinks and wants."[1]

"Less talk and inaccurate assumptions" about one another, if not remedied, will lead eventually to one of these common complaints: "We *don't* communicate;" or "We *can't* communicate," which is most serious because it is perceived as marital failure. In fact, "no communication" has become the catch phrase of the 80s, replacing "mental cruelty" and "incompatibility" as the commonly voiced reason for couples to give up on their marriage.

Why Marriages Fail

In a 1982 survey when four hundred psychiatrists were asked why marriages fail, they gave poor communication as the most common cause.[2] And couples themselves perceive poor communication as the proof that "all is lost." Dr. Renshaw warns,

> Once a couple agrees, "we don't communicate," then they may give up, withdraw emotionally, and conjointly decide that nothing can be done.[3]

Researchers report that most husbands express marital dissatisfaction through anger and *withdrawal,* while most wives show their dissatisfaction through depression and *withdrawal.* In all cases, the withdrawal into silence is devastating and should be regarded as a "red alert" for the marriage.

> The most urgent indicator of distress in a marriage may not be the uproar of discord, but rather the ominous sound of silence, the lack of any communication.[4]

All Is Not Lost

No couple needs to get to that point, however. Any communication problem can be worked out because communication involves skills that can be learned and practiced. In preparation for your first years of forever, we want you to have some advance knowledge of the communication problems that often spring up in marriages and the skills couples need to develop to overcome them.

This may be a good time for you to pause and evaluate the communication system you're now using. Are you and your partner free to express yourselves spontaneously with each other? Are you able to confide in each other as best friends? Or are there difficulties? Do you hear what she's really saying? Do you understand what he's really feeling? Do you share your ideas, thoughts, and feelings? Or do you just talk about practical necessities? Is your communication on practical matters clear enough for things to go smoothly? When you hit a snag in communicating, do you keep on trying until you have overcome the barriers and the flow of meaning opens up between you again? Or do you give up and not try, get angry, yell, or retreat into silence? When you feel rejected, do you retaliate by rejecting your partner?

Checking Out the System

How can you be sure that your communication system is working as it should? Judson Swihart, who also likens communication in marriage to a lifeline, has given five characteristics of a system in good working order:[5]

1. **A sense of freedom to express yourself**
2. **A sense of being understood**
3. **An absence of win-lose arguments**
4. **A reduction of tension**
5. **A sense of being safe and secure in the relationship**

On the other hand, a system that is shut down and critically impaired will manifest these two characteristics:[6]

1. **One or both partners repeatedly assume negative intent on the part of the other.**
2. **There is increasing distance and silence.**

Most people, however, fall somewhere in between with a partially flawed system, which may reflect some, but not all, of the five positive characteristics listed above. Here's how you can build them all into your relationship.

HOW TO BUILD YOUR LIFELINE SYSTEM

---

1. **You will feel free to express yourself when both of you accept one another just as you are.**

Acceptance is the key factor in good communication, for acceptance (or rejection) sends one of the most powerful messages known to human beings. We have an enormous need for unconditional acceptance from the person closest to us. Critical comments or attitudes will make us afraid to express ourselves for fear of being judged. A wife wrote us, "How can I communicate with my husband when he makes a value judgment on everything I say? If he decides it's not worthy of his attention, he quits listening, or he tells me, 'That's not important enough to discuss.' What he's really saying is that *I* am not worth his time and attention."

A critical attitude will also make us want to avoid "intimate talks." A husband said, "Intimate talk means I have to explain why I haven't gotten her vacuum cleaner fixed or why I seem to dislike her mother. My wife enjoys getting things out in the open because, once they're there, I usually have to apologize for them."

Replace a judgmental or fault-finding attitude with a positive response and a consistently accepting attitude, and you will have the ideal climate for a loving interchange of thoughts and feelings. This can lead to the deepening of your love relationship. A young husband, who had been admittedly impatient and somewhat critical, told us, "I have become sensitive to Katie's reaction when I criticize or even show impatience. It seems to be a function of the love God has given me for her that now it hurts me so badly when I see her hurt that I have to back off." He's learning the secret: Good communication *begins* with acceptance.

---

2. You will feel understood when both of you learn to listen with your ears and hearts to one another.

Listening is an important, but often flawed, part of the marital communication system. A specialist in interpersonal communication says,

Even though couples spend over 40% of their communication time listening, it is an underdeveloped skill in most families. Research indicates that we listen at about 25% efficiency, and that much misunderstanding is attributable to poor listening.[7]

Eight Ways to Develop
Your Listening Skills

"Half" Is Not Enough

Make it a practice to give each other your *complete* attention when you talk together. If you only half-listen, you will only half-hear and that's not good enough. Try to listen with your heart as well as your ears to hear what the other is really saying and feeling. Remember that "the human heart holds more than speech does."[8]

No Interruptions

Don't interrupt each other! This can be terribly frustrating for someone trying to put his thoughts and feelings into words. Don't jump to conclusions about what the other is saying. Hear your partner out, then respond.

Repeat, Repeat

Prove that you have listened by repeating your partner's thoughts and feelings back to him so that he is sure you have understood him correctly.

Respond with Your Eyes

Real listening involves concentration accompanied by eye contact. When your partner is sharing thoughts and feelings with you, stop what you're doing and respond with your eyes. Stop and make yourself available when you sense your partner may be wanting to talk.

Don't Wait for Commercial Breaks

Give each other focused attention time with the television turned off. Communication squeezed in during half-time activities or the commercial breaks will be unsatisfying and, even worse, is the effort to talk something over while the television continues to blare and one partner tries to keep an eye on a favorite program. So forego television, put away the video movies, turn off the radio, and shut down the stereo. Close the doors, get your children (if any) occupied elsewhere, and take the telephone off the hook. Never listen with split attention. The communication system of your marriage deserves the very best.

A Negative Feedback Unless. . . .

Remember that your silence can be a negative feedback unless you accompany it with a nonverbal signal of approval, such as a smile, or squeeze of the hand, or loving eye contact.

When the Breakthrough Comes

When there is a breakthrough, never overwhelm your partner by demanding more than he or she is ready to give. Just show appreciation and thankfulness for what has been shared with you. And, of course, never repeat what your partner has told you in confidence.

A Love Message

Remember that when you listen to your partner, you are showing love. You are giving your partner the message, "What you have to say to me is important because *you* are important."

---

3. You will be rid of win-lose arguments in your marriage when you learn what causes them and how to replace them with real communication in resolving disagreements and conflicts.

Why is it that differences of opinion between husband and wife so often lead to arguments and a breakdown in communication? Usually the differences are not life and death matters. They aren't even right and wrong matters. Just different ways of seeing things or handling a situation. At such times the couple's communication skills are tested. Here are some of the ways the conversation may go wrong.

Six Ways a Discussion Goes Wrong

A War to Be Won

The disagreement becomes a war to be won—a power struggle. But the fact is that no one wins in an argument. Your goal should be to win by reaching an agreement or an understanding, while maintaining your good feelings for one another.

A Personal Rejection

The disagreement is taken as a personal rejection. Unfortunately, people often confuse rejection of their ideas with rejection of themselves. You can benefit in marriage from bringing your varying viewpoints together and discussing them, finding a solution, and gaining a deeper appreciation for one another at the same time.

A Change of Weapons

People change the subject and drag in other issues to use as weapons against their partners, instead of limiting the discussion to the original disagreement. As soon as one feels attacked and reacts with defensiveness, communication and loving intimacy are on the way out the door. If you want to avoid this and resolve the issue, agree ahead of time to discuss only the matter at hand. Let the law of kindness be on your tongue. The Bible says that words can pierce like a sword, but the wise tongue brings health and well-being.

Sweeping Generalizations

People, frustrated by their inability to make their point, resort to sweeping generalizations characterized by the use of these expressions: "You *always.* . . ." and "You *never.* . . ." These are "fighting words" and there is almost no adequate response to them. The temptation is to stoop to the same tactic and argue, "I do not! You always. . . ." or "You never. . . ."

Shouting or Siberia

People sometimes respond to disagreements in even more inappropriate and childish ways. One wife wrote us, "I wish my husband could discuss a matter without shouting. He seems to think that talking loud and fast is the only way to communicate." A husband told us, "My only option is to agree with my wife on every point. Otherwise, she sends me to Siberia for weeks at a time."

Yes, But. . . .

People often pull out this prize communication stopper: "Yes, *but.* . . ." which simply escalates the argument. Once we recognize how thoroughly annoying and disheartening this reaction is, we can choose to learn other ways of responding when we disagree. Here's how: Refuse to use those two words in combination again. Learn to make your point differently, beginning with a favorable response, such as "That's an interesting way of looking at it. I hadn't thought of it that way." Or, "I see what you mean." Move right on smoothly into your point, presented as a question, "Do you think that . . . ?"

In other words, present your original reaction in the framework of a measured and respectful response to the other person's idea by taking it seriously. Then tactfully offer your question in such a way that it is not regarded as an attack or a put-down. The discussion begins without ever using a "but," and your partner will feel more like rethinking the issue because you have recognized the validity of his or her position.

All these childish attempts to "win" the disagreement can be changed, if there is a genuine desire to learn to communicate. Excitable people can learn to talk more slowly and calmly, to take deep breaths while they are talking, and to stop to listen. People who pout, who use the deep freeze to express their displeasure, can learn that open, honest discussion has its rewards. Most importantly, marriage partners can learn to appreciate the peace (the restfulness), which comes when they respect one another's right to hold different views and to express those views in a calm discussion.

When a disagreement occurs, it's important to defuse its explosive potential by reducing what's at stake. When your attitude changes from a win/lose, I'm right/you're wrong position to a "Let's talk this over, but it doesn't affect our love and respect for one another" perspective, you've won the real battle. Here are some principles to follow.

Eight Ways to Replace Arguments with Communication

Response, Not Reaction

Don't interrupt. Listen carefully before you respond. Don't react. Respond. Keep the discussion squarely on the issue at hand. You need to agree, long before disagreements arise, that you will limit any discussion to the present, leaving the past out of it, and limit the discussion to the one issue, refusing to allow side issues to enter in.

Disagreement, Not Disapproval

Acknowledge that you understand what your partner is saying, even though you disagree. Show him or her respect. Don't let your disagreement of this issue sound like *disapproval* of your partner.

The Gift of Empathy

Make it a point to share your feelings, but not in such a way that your partner feels criticized. Encourage your partner to share his feelings and respond to them lovingly. Give him or her the gift of sympathy and empathy. This is one way to teach each other to give what you both are longing for.

Carefully Clarify

Carefully clarify what you are both saying so there can be no misunderstanding. Take turns doing this, with no interruptions.

Truthing in Love

Speak the truth in love. The original expression in the New Testament (Eph. 4:15) is literally *truthing in love*—maintaining truth in love, both with your speech and with your behavior. Honesty and love are needed, so speak the truth but speak it gently.

Say "I Need You"

Be willing to show your vulnerable, needy side to your partner. Don't be afraid to say "I need you." Sometimes we want to conceal our feelings to protect ourselves, but when you begin communicating, you learn the value of being honest, even about your own weaknesses. Real communication means revealing yourself even at the risk of rejection. When both are willing to do this, you are well on your way to building loving intimacy in your relationship.

Surprise and Disarm

Stop being defensive when the issue is a personal one. Surprise and disarm your partner by agreeing there is wrong on your side, since there always is (even if you don't wish to admit it). Be specific. "I was wrong" can stop a fight and demonstrate to your partner how to admit wrong, too.

Apply the B-E-S-T

Apply the B-E-S-T principles in your communication. As you talk with each other, *bless* with your words; *edify* (or build up) your partner by what you say and by your interest in what your partner has to say; *share* openly and honestly; and *touch* affectionately while you talk. *Bless, edify, share, and touch*—communicate the BEST to your mate.

---

4. **You can reduce tensions by recognizing and correcting the communication practices that cause frustration and by learning to fight the biblical way—a way that deals constructively with anger, resentment, and hurt feelings.**

RECOGNIZING THE FRUSTRATIONS

We have already mentioned many of the communication practices that cause frustration. Here are five "deadly sins" in communication, which can blight any relationship.

SHUTTING DOWN: Not listening.

SILENT TREATMENT: Not talking.

STABBING: Using the other's words against him/her.

SCOLDING: Putting guilt, blame on the other.

SHALLOW LIMITS: Surface talk only.

When Silence Is a Sin Against Love

We need to take another look at one of these sins against love, for that is what they all are. The "silent treatment" as a punitive measure may be the most hurtful of all. It makes us feel unloved, even despised, and it taps into old childhood fears of being abandoned and helpless. To be shunned by the person we love severs the links of trust, which are so necessary for an intimate relationship. In short, it is one of the most destructive things a person can do to a marriage.

Silence is often used . . . in a power struggle. . . . The withholder often feels powerful for he can manipulate both the feelings and behavior of the other. This is a favorite ploy in the "something-is-wrong-but-I-will-NEVER-tell-you game. Sometimes a fierce competition takes place and the goal is to see who can hurt whom the most. If the competition is in the form of who can be the coldest and most uncommunicative, breaking the silence becomes a sign of weakness. . . .

Silence can be passive-aggressive behavior, which is indirect, covert, and camouflaged hostility. The hostility is never dealt with openly and, therefore, often feeds on itself and becomes greater. Because the silence prevents hostility from being overtly recognized and dealt with, alienation may result, which is more destructive than fighting.[9]

The Messages We Miss

Alienation leads to more alienation. The more distance you've placed, the more likely you are to miss or distort messages transmitted between you. Considering the delicate and complex nature of the hundreds of messages sent and received in a day's time between husband and wife, with words comprising only seven percent of what is communicated, (the rest coming through tone of voice, body language, and even more subtle factors), is it any wonder that misunderstood messages can seriously damage an already shaky relationship?

The Five-Second Pause

Take this example: The wife asks her husband, "Do you really love me?" The husband waits five seconds and answers, "Of course I do." Every woman knows the important part of that message: the five-second pause. It changes the husband's answer from reassuring to ambiguous and unsatisfying.

The Silence of a Closed Door

There is another sort of painful silence when a partner will not go beyond shallow conversation. It is the silence of a closed door. When this silence refuses the other one's entrance to his heart, their relationship becomes empty, seemingly dead in the water.

> To be silent about one's deepest feelings in a marriage often leads to a dead space in which there is nothing to communicate.[10]

This problem will require loving persistence, patience, and prayer, but unconditional love does have power to open doors. The reward for both partners will be a growing and deepening love as they allow themselves to become known without self-imposed barriers.

Other Frustrations

Here are some other frustrating communication practices.

1. Pretending you are communicating, when you're merely attacking your spouse.

2. Not knowing how to express your feelings without putting each other down.

3. Stating your views as though they are the absolute truth. (There's the old proverb, *One who is too insistent on his own views finds few to agree with him.*)

4. Not hearing the message from your partner because you're too busy figuring out what to say next. You can take it as a general rule that you will never be able to send messages successfully unless you are also paying attention to receiving them.

5. Faking attention, but not really listening. This is dangerous business. Faking attention with a glassy-eyed stare while you're thinking of something else will trip you up, and your partner will be understandably insulted. Researchers say that good listening is accompanied by a slight rise in temperature, a faster heartbeat, and a quicker circulation of blood. In other words, listening is not a passive activity! You should establish eye contact, think while listening, and not only concentrate on the words, but observe the nonverbal behavior of the speaker. All of this must be integrated into the meaning of the message.

6. Trying to communicate when you have two different goals for the conversation.

For example, when a wife pours out her problem to her husband, she may not be looking for an instant solution. Her husband, who views himself as a problem solver, gives her a quick way to handle the problem, and then becomes frustrated when she does not appreciate his brilliant solution. She's equally frustrated because she needed just to talk with him about it and to feel his support and understanding. But he says, "Okay, if you don't want my help and don't want to take my advice, then don't talk to me about it." So they are both disappointed. She wants to be listened to and empathized with. He wants to be respected for his ability and smart thinking. Neither is getting what he or she wants!

It's best to know the initial purpose of the conversation. The one who is being approached should be sensitive to the other's needs and goals for the conversation. If necessary, ask in a tactful way. Body language, tone of voice, and facial expressions will tell you a great deal.

Usually, the wife will be more relationally oriented, and the husband more data oriented. He doesn't realize how short he sounds when he asks where the tax file is. He just wants to know to get the job done. She is more concerned about relating to her lover and feels surprised and wounded by the curt, businesslike edge to his voice. The result may be a minor crisis in which fence-mending, for that night at least, becomes more urgent than filing the tax form.

This illustrates one of the most frustrating areas of communication in marriage: the difference between men and women.

7. Husband and wife communicate differently, and this can lead to misunderstandings and mutual exasperation.

At a national seminar session on communication, the speaker suggested that men are outclassed when it comes to verbal facility. Women talk better. They develop the language earlier and are more skillful in its use.

He also said men are more linear in their thinking, moving from a to b to c, while a woman can surround the subject from nine directions. And she is usually more concerned with "people" issues.

The speaker said he had discovered firsthand from his wife that women will repeat the same thing several times to their husbands because to share it you have to say it several times. He added that men do the same thing, but they say it to three different people!

One significant difference to keep in mind is the way men and women use the words *want* and *need*. Women don't mind saying, "I need," and may say it often. Men do not. To express need makes many men uncomfortable. When they say anything, it's usually "I want." Wives need to remember that men have needs, whether or not they are willing to express them.

8. Cultural differences and personality differences also take their toll on patience. In the pressure cooker of marriage, the cool Swede from Rockford, Illinois, may seem too cold for comfort to his Italian wife from south St. Louis. And the girl he loved because she was so vivacious and delightfully unpredictable becomes "noisy and undependable" instead.

Even if you came from similar backgrounds, you will be surprised at the differences, which emerge and the adaptations that are necessary. Strong clashes are inevitable between two people who love each other, but the Bible shows husbands and wives how to deal with their anger, resentments, and hurt feelings constructively.

Learning to Fight the Biblical Way

In Strike the Original Match, Charles R. (Chuck) Swindoll says that Ephesians 4:25–32 "offers seven rules for having a good fight. These rules will allow you to carry on normal, natural, disagreeable times without breaking with Scripture." Here are Chuck Swindoll's *Rules on How to Keep It Clean* from Ephesians 4:25–32.

1. **Keep it honest (v. 25).** Be committed to honesty and mutual respect.
2. **Keep it under control (v. 26).** Make sure your weapons are not deadly.
3. **Keep it timed right (vs. 26–27).** Agree together that the time is right to talk.
4. **Keep it positive (v. 28).** Be ready with a positive solution right after taking a swing.
5. **Keep it tactful (v. 29).** Watch your words and guard your tongue.
6. **Keep it private (v. 31).** Don't swing at your mate in public. When you swing in public, your malice is showing.

7. **Keep it cleaned up (v. 32).** When it's all over, help clean up the mess.[11]

We encourage you to study these "rules" and make them a part of your new life together. They are practical; they are wise; they work! They can guide you through your conflicts in a controlled, constructive way that hurts neither of you and actually causes you to love each other more, after "the fight" is over.

---

5. **You will feel safe and secure in your relationship if you get to know one another through good communication and remain closely in touch for a lifetime.**

Think about this rather melancholy statement spoken by the Duke of Wellington at the end of his life in 1852:

"It's a strange thing that two people can live together for half a lifetime and only understand one another at the very end."

Does it have to be that way? Definitely not. At the conclusion of this chapter we'll share the story of two people who understood each other most of their lives because they communicated all along the way. Their story is a reminder that you can build a lifeline system of loving, unhindered communication that will make it possible for you to become

- Intimate lovers
- Best friends who always enjoy being together
- A team that can accomplish anything because you work together rather than fighting for control
- Two people who understand one another as unique

individuals, not as extensions of yourselves, and accept each other just as you are
- A couple who stay in touch during the changes of a lifetime, who "grow up together" and "grow old together" and remain "at home" with each other no matter what else changes
- Compassionate partners who can help one another adjust to the difficult times of life and endure them together

Now that's security!

GUARDING YOUR LIFELINE

Security takes a bit of guarding. In your case, you will know more than anyone else about the sensitive points in your relationship, which need special watchfulness. Here are our suggestions.

Six Warnings for Lovers

Be Alert to Unusual Tension.

Be sensitive to the danger when an uncomfortable tension is felt concerning some topic. Nothing does more harm to a good marriage than the rising of invisible walls because of something that cannot be talked about together. The caring may remain, but the intimacy and trust depart.

Therapists name *loss of effective communication* as the most common cause of distress in a previously stable marriage.[12] When some kind of distress cuts the lines that unite you, you must take quick action to resolve the situation.

Never Betray Your Best Friend.

Be on guard against taking something shared with you in a vulnerable moment and turning it against your mate as a weapon. This is easy to do when you're angry, feeling condemned, and fighting back. But as one husband said, "If you get into a revenge mode of thinking, it's like trying to stop a moving train." NEVER give way to the temptation. Remember, this is the person you want for your best friend.

Beware of the Heat of the Moment.

This is another "heat of the moment" danger. When you have a confrontation (and you will) about something so significant that you both become overwrought, you may say too much—something you'd give anything to take back later. But it's too late then. So have the good sense to stop and cool it when you recognize you're getting to that point. Go in separate rooms for a short time, and write down your feelings just as they are. Then come back together with the intensity of the moment dissipated, remembering that, no matter what, this is your intimate lover whom you don't want to wound, or lose.

It's good to make Psalm 141:3 your prayer and to pray it together before talking: "Set a watch, O Lord, before my mouth; keep the door of my lips."

Never Look at Your Mate Without Compassion.

Never close your heart to your loved one, even in the heat of the moment. To see your *one flesh* partner without feeling compassion is unthinkable. To see your partner in need and not pity him or her is to be without love. The principle—one of the most important you can learn for your marriage—is " We know love by this, that He laid down His life for us; and we ought to lay down our lives for the brethren. But whoever has the world's goods, and beholds his brother in need and closes his heart against him, how does the love of God abide in him? Little children, let us not love with word or with tongue, but in deed and truth" (John 3:16–18 NASV).

First, we are to be willing to lay down our lives for one of our own. To "lay down" means to divest ourselves of something that is part of us, for instance, our selfish desires. We are to love as He loved us. His love is to pour through us and touch others, especially the one closest to us, our own marriage partner. We are to give definite form to the love of Jesus Christ and show it by example. This kind of love reveals itself in details, in acts of behavior, attitude, small words, little smiles, as well as enormous acts of self-giving, done in such a way that there is no hint of martyrdom. If your partner feels you are sacrificing, something is wrong with the way you are showing your love.

Second, we are not to close our heart against a loved one's need. To look at our mate without *splanchna* (pity) is not love. That pity is a deep-seated emotional concern and affectionate sympathy. We must *feel*. Jesus was moved with compassion. He was torn up. He wept, He felt compassion. We need to emerge from our self-centeredness and affirm our solidarity with our partner. We need to open our inner life and feel deeply for and with our mate.

The award-winning movie *Ordinary People* portrayed an outwardly charming woman who is unwilling to open herself inwardly to her husband and son at the time of their deepest needs. They desperately want her compassion, some outward sign of her caring, but she cannot or will not give it. Defeated in his efforts to reach her, her husband says sadly, "I don't know you. I don't know what we've been playing at all this time." He adds, "We could have done all right if there had been no mess in our life." But all lives have "messes." We all need compassion from our partner.

So, thirdly, we must act. Not just love with our words— with our tongue that says pleasant things when we're in the right mood—but in *deed* (action) and truth. That should be our response to the compassion we feel.

Remember the Power of Words.

Remember what power your words have to affect your partner's life. Sometimes we discount their potent influence. Emily Dickinson put it this way,

> A word is dead
> When it is said,
> Some say.
>
> I say it just
> Begins to live
> That day.[13]

Our words have the power to penetrate another person's inner being, and their effects spread outward in a way that seems almost unending. Who can say where a word ends? Here is Derek Kidner's explanation:

1. *Penetration.* What is done to you is of little account beside what is done *in* you. . . . The *feelings,* or morale, may be lacerated by a cruel or clumsy thrust . . . or vitalized by a timely word . . . and the whole body with them. . . . *Beliefs and convictions* are formed by words, and these either destroy a man or are the making of him.

2. *Spread.* Since words implant ideas in other minds, their effects ramify—again, for good or evil.[14]

Our words can wound or heal; weaken or strengthen; depress or inspire; drive to despair or fill with happiness. It's particularly hard to overcome their negative impact. The injurious effects of words once spoken suggests that we sometimes communicate all too clearly. Our partner has no difficulty in receiving the message of our anger, disappointment, and complete dissatisfaction! "Everyone should be quick to listen, slow to speak and slow to become angry" (James 1:19 NIV). Or, "Consider what a great forest is set on fire by a small spark. The tongue also is a fire. . . ." (James 3:5–6b NIV).

If you want to enhance your "word power" and harness

it for good, we recommend studying the Book of Proverbs. Make a study together of biblical principles of communication, taking all the verses in Proverbs about this, one at a time, and applying them in your marriage. Here are some to get you started.

Proverbs 12:18 There is one who speaks rashly like the thrusts of a sword, but the tongue of the wise brings healing.

Proverbs 15:1 A gentle answer turns away wrath, but a harsh word stirs up anger.

Proverbs 18:13 He who gives an answer before he hears, it is folly and shame to him.

Watch Out for the Third Partner in Your Marriage.

For at least fifteen years Dr. Wheat urged newlyweds to begin their marriage without a television set in the house. Young people sometimes thought that was asking too much. Now, couples are realizing what a thief television can be, robbing them of their prime time together. A bride told Gloria recently, "We decided not to get a TV, and it's been wonderful. There's nothing else to do but spend time paying attention to each other!"

Even television's voice, *TV Guide,* questions whether TV can cause divorce. Psychiatrist David Hellerstein observes that today

the TV *itself,* that noisy box in the corner of the living room, has become an equal—and essential—partner in many marriages. Even when it's turned off, there's that blank screen waiting to rejoin the conversation or to monopolize one's—or worse, one's spouse's–attentions.

Then Hellerstein asks a pointed question that every newly-married couple, interested in good communication, needs to consider.

Is there any connection between the fact that so many marriages now have three partners (two human, one

75

electronic) and the fact that more than one million American couples now divorce every year? Consider that so much TV viewing occurs in early evening—which, as Miriam Arond points out, ''is the time of day that couples are most in need of communication.' Does the silent ''conversation'' with the TV set replace invaluable human communication?

He concludes,

At worst, TV can be an escape from problems that desperately need to be dealt with directly. And an ''affair'' with TV watching can kill a marriage. The fast pace and slickness of the TV world can, as Miriam Arond says, ''promote unrealistic expectations of passionate romance, that life should have a pace of passion that your own life doesn't have.'' One result is ''that people are less good at weathering problems than they were in the old days'' and the quick fixes suggested by many TV shows can reinforce one's impulse to get out fast.[15]

Whatever conclusions you reach about the part TV should have in your marriage, whether as third partner or infrequent guest, we trust you will see good communication as such a vital part of your love relationship, (so hard-won and so easily lost!) that you will guard it to the utmost.

Two people who did this were close friends of ours: John and Richie Wadsworth. For forty eventful years this couple communicated, and when John was diagnosed as having cancer, they were able to support one another through that experience, too. Richie wrote about it afterward, and we asked if we could share it with our readers who are just beginning their journey together.

"I Love You, John"

The seven weeks from the diagnosis of cancer to those last moments when the breath came more and more slowly, and finally not at all, was a vast learning experience and a spiritual growing period for both of us.

Basically we were the same persons who had, for forty years of marriage, been together, laughed, teased, made decisions, argued, agreed, and cried together. We had stubbornly said, "I love you," even when we didn't like each other much. We had said it passionately, contentedly, reassuringly, proudly, and "just because."

Communication was open when cancer invaded our lives, because communication had been kept open during our years of marriage.

Illness didn't change our ability to laugh and kid around. We reminisced lots. We cried unashamedly. Most of all, we communicated every thought we had. Fear was never present because Christ was the center of our lives and He had removed fear on the cross for us. We marveled at that.

Sometimes the medicine gave John fantasies as he slept; usually they were not disturbing ones, but mostly he would be traveling. One day he said, "It is so strange, but I was on this trip and in this house that was mine, and yet not this one; and in this room that was mine, and yet not this one—"

I interrupted, "Well, you're going to be taking a trip and—" Together we said, "In my Father's house are many mansions . . . I go to prepare a place for you."

Communication made our last days together rich. If it hadn't been building through the years it wouldn't have been there for us to enjoy in the last days of our life together.

In the middle of the night, Friday, I came back in the room with fresh water. When John heard the ice tinkle in the glass he turned his head and smiled. I said, "Hey, I love you."

He groped for my hand with his left hand, because by this time the bone in his right arm had disintegrated, pulled my hand to his lips and said, "I love you, too. Oh, my, yes!"

I had prayed so much that John would not lose his ability to speak and God had granted my desire. We had talked about the fact that if we hadn't been open and loving all these years, the last days of our life would have been too late to start.

Saturday and Sunday, the voice I loved became a whisper, but still I communicated, and as I held his hand and his quiet breathing stopped, he stepped over the threshold and I was saying, "I love you, John."

6

The Door Marked Private:
Secrets of Sexual Fulfillment

Therefore shall a man leave his father and his mother, and shall cleave unto his wife; and they shall be one flesh. And they were both naked, the man and his wife, and were not ashamed (Gen. 2:24–25).

"May my beloved come into his garden, and eat its choice fruits!"

"I have come into my garden, my sister, my bride. I have gathered my myrrh along with my balsam. I have eaten my honeycomb and my honey; I have drunk my wine and my milk."

(God to the Couple) Eat, friends; drink and imbibe deeply, O lovers" (Song of Sol. 4:16, 5:1 NASV).

When you feel an overwhelming sexual desire for each another, you can lock out the rest of the world without guilt or shame and express your love physically in total freedom. That's the wonder of marriage!

But there's more. God promises that through sexual union the two of you will become *one flesh*. Real love causes us to long to be as close to the beloved as possible, and God's provision is to meet that longing. The term *one flesh* means the merging of your personalities, the sharing of your entire beings so that you can really know each other. In fact, the biblical word for sexual intercourse is to

"know." "Adam knew Eve his wife; and she conceived"
(Gen. 4:1). "Then Joseph . . . took unto him his wife: and
knew her not until she had brought forth her firstborn son"
(Matt. 1:24–35).

So, never think of sex as an extra added attraction. It is
meant to be at the very heart of your marriage, becoming
the most private and priceless expression of your love in
the sharing of all that you are with one another.

Here's the way one wife described the relationship.
Susan explained,

> Sex in our marriage has been a magic thread which sews us
> together into one person. Even after the lovemaking is over,
> the thread still holds in this magical way, and we go about
> our ordinary life smiling at each other with satisfaction,
> sitting down together to our pasta salad with a special
> quality of contentment, knowing that we know each other
> fully and love each other completely. It's a secret delight
> that we share—or maybe I mean a delightful secret.

> Anyway, sharing this secret knowledge with the man I love
> is an important part of it: the private looks, the private
> smiles, the private meanings in what we say. It's our time to
> recapture the feeling of being young and in love. It keeps us
> in touch with that secret place we discovered ten years ago.
> Now we have kids to raise, bikes in the driveway, bills to
> pay, schedules and interruptions, and all kinds of demands
> on our time and thoughts. But at night when the house is
> quiet, we can retreat back into our private world and
> imprint our oneness on our hearts again.

> One benefit of what I call the magic thread is that the good
> effects don't last. It's not a once for all thing; we are drawn
> back to each other again and again. We just can't do without
> our reunions. I don't see how any marriage can survive
> without those times when you can concentrate on each
> other, and shut the rest of the world out!

It's true from Day One of your marriage into "forever."
Some of you are engaged couples preparing for your

wedding and honeymoon. Others are newlyweds who have been married long enough to want a different set of questions answered. Some of you may be building a second marriage and bringing the sexual experiences of your first marriage into this one. Or you may have had sex with various people and wonder how this will affect your relationship in marriage. Since we want to speak to all of you and your circumstances, let's begin with biblical counsel about sex—guidelines about how to enjoy sex in marriage from the Inventor of all good pleasures and conclude with the secrets of sexual fulfillment, which every couple needs to know.

BIBLICAL COUNSEL

1. Approach sex with reverence because you know what it means.

If you're clear on this first point, you can avoid the wrong attitudes toward sex that create such deep heartaches in marriages. For example, we have seen many fearful, inhibited people who believe that sex between husbands and wives is something to be ashamed of. Even as Queen Victoria wrote to her daughter, "The animal side of our nature is to me—to dreadful." At the other end of the spectrum, we counsel couples where one of the partners holds a cheap, casual view of sex with self-centered, physical gratification as the only goal, as a "whatever-turns-you-on" encounter. People from both these extremes share a common misunderstanding: They believe that sex is an expression of the animal nature.

If you feel that you are veering toward either extreme in your attitudes toward sex, you can correct your course and safeguard your love relationship with these biblical facts as fixed points in your understanding.

When God originated sexuality, He called it very good.

So God created man in his own image, in the image of God created he him; male and female created he them. And God blessed them, and God said unto them, Be fruitful, and multiply and fill the earth. . . . And God saw every thing that he had made, and, behold, it was very good (Gen. 1:27, 28, 31).

The word "man" (*adam,* not a proper name) denotes two sexual beings made for intimate union with each other. If you read Genesis 1, you'll see that all other parts of creation had been pronounced "good." It was not until man and woman were created as sexual beings endowed with the mysterious qualities and attributes of masculinity and femininity that God called his creation "very good." Also note that God's first word to his new creatures was a command to exercise their sexuality.

God sees sex in marriage as pure and valuable.

Marriage is honorable in all, and the bed undefiled, but fornicators and adulterers God will judge (Heb. 13:4).

The New Testament teaches that sex was not only good at its origin, but when enjoyed in the context of marriage according to the Creator's design, it is highly valuable and beautifully pure. We explained the meaning of Hebrews 13:4 in a secular textbook for college students.

Three words require special attention. The word translated as "honorable" means most precious, costly, of great price. The word translated "bed" is, literally, coitus—a plain reference to sexual intercourse. And the word "undefiled" signifies freedom from contamination—purity. In one cogent sentence, the Bible says that marriage—God's chosen environment for the expression of sexuality—is most precious, of indescribable value, and that sexual intercourse in that setting is so pure that it could take place (and does!) as an act of worship.[1]

This scripture depicts the marriage bed as a sort of "holy of holies" where husband and wife meet privately to celebrate their love for each other. But if sex is holy in that setting, it is no less enjoyable physically. We were created as sensual beings with piercing desires, and our bodies were intricately designed to experience exquisite sexual pleasures. The Bible places high value on the human body for its own sake as "wonderfully made" by the Creator (Ps. 139:14) and inhabited by the incarnate Savior. The same body that enters into the passionate, physical delights of intercourse with one's marriage partner is described as "the temple of the Holy Spirit" (1 Cor. 6:19).[1]

Obviously, we can't uphold this truth and ignore the other side of it. The same verse from Hebrews that assures us of the worth and purity of sexual intercourse in marriage warns us against contaminating God's good gift by engaging in sexual intercourse outside of marriage.

Many of the couples who contact us are having difficulties because of guilt, even when their premarital sex was with one another. If you have violated God's plan for enjoyment of your sexuality please remember that God can forgive, cleanse, heal, and restore. A missionary/teacher offers this good advice.

You can have a great marriage and future, so don't despair. I've heard women who were once prostitutes say that on their wedding night it felt like the first time. God can do a mighty work in your life! Come to Him and admit that He really knew what He was talking about, and you were wrong to second-guess Him. Repent and then by faith let Him reverse the damage. . . . Let Him direct the river of your sexuality as a river within its banks, and it will become a thing of beauty and fulfillment in your life.[2]

Sex in the environment of permanent commitment in marriage has profound meaning and a spiritual purpose.

For we are members of his body, of his flesh, and of his bones. For this cause shall a man leave his father and mother, and shall be joined unto his wife, and they two shall be one flesh. This is a great mystery, but I speak concerning Christ and the church (Ephes. 5:30–32).

The Book of Ephesians reveals that the one-flesh union of husband and wife is intended to picture the intimate closeness, total commitment, and permanent love relationship that Jesus Christ has for the church. This puts the sexual relationship of marriage in its true perspective. It is never sinful to love your partner sexually and passionately; it is never meaningless to engage in sexual intercourse with your own mate. Real pleasure begins when you approach your sexual lovemaking with the reverent respect it deserves.

2. Enjoy sex as recreation because God planned it that way.

When you understand the true meaning of sexual intercourse, you're ready to appreciate the delights God has prepared for you in marriage. As we explained in *Intended for Pleasure,*

Sex with your partner is far more than recreation, of course, but it is that as well: the best, the most relaxing, renewing recreation known to man, and God planned that too. No wonder it is often called "love play." It is fun, not duty; high excitement, not boredom; something to anticipate, not a dreary experience to be avoided if you can. It should be and it can be the highlight of any ordinary day, as two people come together to refresh themselves in each other's love, to find forgetfulness from the cares and insults of life, and to experience the total and wonderful relaxation God designed as the culmination of the lovemaking, with both husband and wife reaching release. How ironic that couples search for all manner of recreation elsewhere, never having discovered the fullness of pleasure available to them in their own bedroom.[3]

Read and reread together the Song of Solomon in a modern translation, and apply it to your own love affair. You will find that the sexual relationship of your marriage can provide refreshment, restoration, joy, liberty, and an abundance of delights. And not just now while you are newlyweds! Hear the counsel from the Book of Proverbs, which specializes in down-to-earth wisdom for the situations of life. The theme of Proverbs 5 could be summed up this way: Stay away from people who would lure you into unfaithfulness and always be madly in love with your own wife. Here is a clear description of the sexual pleasures in a lifetime marriage, "Let thy fountain be blessed, and rejoice with the wife of thy youth. Let her be as the loving hind and pleasant roe; let her breasts satisfy thee at all times, and be thou ravished always with her love" (Prov. 5:18–19).

The wife is pictured, both here and in Song of Solomon, as a well, a spring shut up, a fountain sealed for her husband, whose waters will satisfy him to the fullest. To be satisfied, in the Hebrew language, means to have one's thirst slaked, to take one's fill, to be abundantly saturated with that which pleases. And to be ravished with love means to be enraptured . . . intoxicated . . . exhilarated.

The verses from Song of Solomon quoted at the beginning of this chapter describe the consummation of love on the wedding night. S. Craig Glickman calls it "one of the shyest and most delicate of love scenes in world literature." Afterward, the husband describes their love as a beautiful garden he has enjoyed and as a great feast he has celebrated.

Nevertheless, the words of the lovers are not the last words of the night. A mysterious voice is the last to speak. "Eat, O loved ones; drink and be drunk, O lovers." (Song of Sol.

5:1B) Who is speaking to the lovers here? Some have suggested the wedding guests, but of course they are not likely to be around at this moment. And neither is any other person for that matter. Yet the voice must represent someone other than the lovers, for they are the ones addressed here. . . .

In the final analysis this must be the voice of the Creator, the greatest Poet, the most intimate wedding guest of all, the one, indeed, who prepared this lovely couple for the night of his design.

He lifts his voice and gives hearty approval to the entire night. He vigorously endorses and affirms the love of this couple. He takes pleasure in what has taken place. He is glad they have drunk deeply of the fountain of love. Two of his own have experienced love in all the beauty and fervor and purity that he intended for them. In fact, he urges them on to more. . . . Eat together from the feast I have prepared for you. This is his attitude toward the giving of their love to each other.

And by the way, that's also his attitude toward couples today.[4]

3. Recognize your responsibility to your mate.

In 1 Corinthians 7, we are offered four valuable guidelines for the expression of sex in marriage—all of which emphasize responsibility to one another as lovers.

The Principle of Need

But since there is so much immorality, each man should have his own wife, and each woman her own husband. The husband should fulfill his marital duty to his wife, and likewise the wife to her husband (1 Cor. 7:2–3 NIV).

The first principle is simple: The two of you *need* the blessings and protection of sex within your marriage. It's important for you to do everything you can to meet your partner's needs. If both of you take hold of this concept and live it out, the result will be a tender, but very exciting relationship.

The Principle of Belonging

The wife's body does not belong to her alone but also to her husband. In the same way, the husband's body does not belong to him alone but also to his wife (1 Cor. 7:4 NIV).

The second principle is less simple and very sobering. When two people marry, they relinquish ownership of their own bodies and give this right to their mate. Obviously, this requires the utmost trust. People should understand before they marry that when they do, in God's sight, they will belong sexually to each other and will have no right to withhold physical affection. Bluntly speaking, the wife's body now belongs to her husband; the husband's body now belongs to his wife. However, each must love the other's body and care for it as his own. Unreasonable demands are totally excluded.

The Principle of Habit

Do not deprive each other except by mutual consent and for a time, so that you may devote yourselves to prayer. Then come together again so that Satan will not tempt you because of your lack of self-control (1 Cor. 7:5 NIV).

The third principle uses a harsh word, "Deprive," *apostereo,* which actually means to rob or defraud one another. In other words, don't cheat your partner by withholding habitual sexual lovemaking except by mutual consent for a brief period of time. If you do, you will open your marriage to satanic temptations. Our Creator knows this. That's why He counsels us to participate actively and regularly in sex with our own mates.

The Principle of Equality

This principle comes from the passage we have been quoting and finds its best illustration in the relationship of the lovers in Song of Solomon. Sexual relations are to be equal and reciprocal; each has the right to initiate sex, and neither has the right to use it as a bargaining point.

The husband and wife are *equals*. Their sexual relationship has been designed for two equals—a man and woman permanently committed to marriage—who love, not use, one another. A science fiction novel a few years ago portrayed a futuristic society in which couples are no longer called lovers but *users*. Television reflects a trend toward this chilling future: In one survey of American television, researchers reported that 88 percent of all sex presented on television was sex outside of marriage—people using other people for momentary gratification.

The biblical principles for the enjoyment of sex totally contradict this approach. God's counsel concerning sex advises us to be always loving and concerned for the welfare and happiness of each other. Let's hear again from Susan who told us about the "magic thread." We asked her how she and Don had maintained such a beautiful relationship in their ten-year-old marriage. Her answer shows the biblical guidelines in action.

We follow three simple rules, not laws, but ways of communicating love. First, we keep our sex life separate from our quarrels and disagreements. That's not as hard as it sounds. Our sex life is so good; we don't want any harm to come to it, so we protect that private place, and neither one of us drags other things in. When we fight, we make up; then we make love. We have never in ten years of marriage used sex against one another.

Second, we're almost always available for one another. When one's in the mood, the other reciprocates and soon gets in the mood. Of course, we don't make demands when we know our partner is tired or sick or upset. That's just good manners and thoughtfulness.

Third, if one of us just isn't up to it, we ask to postpone it for another time in a way that sounds like loving anticipation, not like rejection. We've always related this way sexually, and a few years ago when we began studying the Bible, we found that by some miracle of love, we had done things right!

4. Remember the privacy factor.
Becoming one flesh in marriage calls for privacy in every sense of the word. Here are some ways to apply this in your relationship.
Don't let another person intrude into your private world for two.
This is one part of your life where close friends, children, and beloved family members do not belong! *Private* means not for common use, secluded, removed from public view.
Beware of the invader—an individual who would like to take your partner's place in your life.
To allow a close friendship marked by affectionate touching and intimate conversation to grow is like leaving the gate open and inviting that person into your heart as a lover.
Avoid family members, friends, or neighbors who encourage you to talk about your partner until you see yourself separately from him or her.
Guard your sense of oneness. It's precious.
Never discuss details of your sexual relationship with anyone except a physician or counselor, if it becomes necessary.
Your sex life should be viewed as sacred. Never permit jokes about your private world or share confidences with others in this sensitive area.
Establish and maintain the privacy of your bedroom.
Keep a lock on your bedroom door and use it. Children

should be trained from a very young age to knock on Mother and Daddy's door, never to barge in. Do not allow your children to sleep with you or in the same room with you. When you buy or build a home, try to obtain a master bedroom arrangement that offers as much privacy and quiet as possible. Your bedroom should be a sanctuary of love. Make it beautiful, keep it pleasant, and use it only for sleeping, dressing, and relating as lovers.

BEFORE THE WEDDING NIGHT COUNSEL

It's good that you are preparing now for the physical dimension of your marriage, even though it may be some weeks before your wedding. The sexual relationship involves far more than doing what comes naturally, and no one should feel that he has to be an instant expert. For a new husband to have to pretend that he knows it all can be quite a burden. No one knows it all. Even the therapists in the field are continually researching the subject of sexual response, and new facts are coming to light out of this research. God's physical design for sex between husband and wife is beautiful but intricate, and you need to understand the mechanisms of sexual expression and response to prevent difficulties from arising that could hinder your pleasure and rob you of fulfillment.

Many problems can be avoided if you have the right information ahead of time so that you can begin your marriage with positive experiences in lovemaking, and even enjoy sex on your honeymoon—a time that, frankly, is disappointing for couples who have gone into it unprepared or misinformed. Many of the sex problems treated at the Wheat Clinic can be traced back to a honeymoon which was fearful for the bride and frustrating for the groom. This first experience often leads to an habitual state of disappointment, blundering, and boredom in the bedroom. The wife begins to avoid sex altogether, and the husband's hurt turns to anger.

We want you not only to have a wonderful time together on your wedding night, but to gain the confidence that your sex life will get better and better as you practice communicating physically and discover many special ways to please one another. No one can tell you all you need to know about loving your own partner sexually. Only you can develop this knowledge as you become sensitive to your partner's desires. In fact, it is this sensitivity and desire to give pleasure to your partner that will make you a great lover. You need to begin with mental preparation for your wedding night.

1. Do not expect complete physical harmony right away. Be realistic in your expectations. To avoid disappointment, plan your wedding night together ahead of time, each sharing your secret dreams.

On the wedding night, romance and realism meet at the crossroads. Hopefully, they will become compatible and travel together from then on. Nothing is more realistic and "earthy"than sexual intercourse. But what about the romantic dreams. and the idealism that desires a beautiful experience, and the longing for spiritual union which at least one of you may bring to your wedding night? These are just as valid and just as important as the rapture and passion that the other one may be visualizing.

You do need to communicate your desires. Please do not count on your partner to know what you want without being told. Husband, you will have the opportunity of demonstrating your love for your bride by making this a beautiful night, which she will never forget, as well as fulfilling her romantic dreams and enjoying loving physical intimacy. Probably, the first few weeks of sexual encounters will require maximum self-control on the husband's part to allow his wife maximum comfort.

2. Do not be goal-oriented in your lovemaking.

This is particularly directed to the man, since he would tend to judge himself as a lover solely on the basis of whether he is able to bring his bride to sexual release through orgasm. But don't make this the supreme goal of your honeymoon.

Your goal setting and striving to meet that goal puts pressure on your bride to respond and perform properly, but it can have the opposite effect. She will reach orgasm only in a relaxed atmosphere after emotional as well as physical arousal have occurred, and enough skillful physical stimulation has taken place. When she feels pressured by *your* expectation, *her* fear of failure can hinder the physical response she otherwise would have. It can even sensitize her and inhibit her response in the future.

Your purpose on the wedding night should be to develop emotional intimacy through physical closeness. You have new avenues for demonstrating how much you adore your wife, how beautiful you think she is, and how she is the most desirable of women. If you lack imagination, study the Song of Solomon, which describes a thrilling wedding night for both bride and bridegroom.

Concentrate on pleasing your wife with romantic words and gestures, warmth and tenderness, and caressing her entire body in a leisurely manner, which indicates how much you delight in her. Some hasty mechanical fondling of the breasts or genitals as a means of fast arousal is just not the mark of a real lover. Your lovemaking should be leisurely, but purposeful to be exciting, and the excitement should steadily intensify. Begin slowly, enjoying every sensation and every sign of your partner's pleasure, then build gradually to an emotional as well as physical climax. As we explained in *LOVE LIFE,*

Husbands who are preoccupied with physical gratification should know that even for their own maximum enjoyment of sexual release, they need to have at least twenty minutes of sexual arousal beforehand. We some times call orgasm a climax and it should be just that: the highest point of interest and excitement in a series of happenings. How do you reach the high point? By climbing to it. Climax is a Greek word meaning "ladder." You move to a climax with a slow, progressive build-up resulting at the highest point in a sudden, thrilling release—something like a rollercoaster ride with its long, slow climb and then its exciting plunge downward from the peak.[5]

This does require self-control on a young husband's part, but his patience will be rewarded with a fulfilling sex life for many years to come.

Don't be disconcerted if you ejaculate before you want on your wedding night. This might be expected because of your intense feelings. It may happen the moment the penis enters the vagina or even while you are still caressing your bride to bring her to arousal. But this is by no means the end of the lovemaking experience. On your honeymoon another ejaculation will probably appear in a few minutes. Continue to bring your wife to sexual release through stimulation of the clitoris. Actually, this may be more pleasing to her because the vaginal muscles will be very tense, and intercourse will bring some discomfort.

This counsel applies to you even if you have been married before or if you have had previous sexual experiences outside marriage. No matter what's in the past, approach your wedding night as though it were the first time for both of you. This is a fresh start by God's grace and should be handled that way. Treat your bride as gently as though she were a virgin and forget that she is not. Besides, sex within the commitment of marriage is profoundly different from a casual coupling outside of marriage. As one person told us, it's like the contrast between a clear, starry night on a mountain peak and the city smog down in the valley. So enjoy!

Here is some important physical preparation you need to make.

3. Plan the right environment for your honeymoon.

The Old Testament law made provision for a newly-married couple to enjoy a one-year honeymoon. Deuteronomy 24:5 says, "When a man hath taken a new wife, he shall not go out to war, neither shall he be charged with any business: but he shall be free at home one year, and shall cheer up his wife which he hath taken." The Hebrew word translated to cheer up means *to delight his wife and to understand what is exquisitely pleasing to her in the sexual relationship.* Obviously, God gives this top priority.

If your budget has several thousand dollars allocated for your wedding with a hundred dollars left over for an overnight honeymoon, we encourage you to balance your funds so that you can be free of responsibility for a few weeks while you have time to get to know each other. During that period, you will have clearer communication lines than you may ever have again. If you miss this opportunity, you may find those communication lines becoming progressively blocked as time goes by.

We recommend that you emphasize comfortable privacy during your honeymoon rather than an elaborate trip. Certainly you should be apart from family and friends. Try to stay in a place where room service will bring meals to your room when requested. Come to your wedding night as rested as possible and do not plan a long drive to your hotel or motel for that first night.

Some thought needs to be given to proper lighting in your bedroom. Since men prefer light and women usually prefer darkness, the best compromise is dim, romantic lighting, which will enhance your lovemaking. Some people take candles with them for subdued lighting.

Also a word about sleepwear. The bride will have some beautiful nightwear; in fact, this may be a part of her romantic dreams. It is best, however, if sometime during the first night you are "naked and unashamed" with one another.

4. Come prepared with an artificial lubricant. This is an essential.

Plenty of lubrication is a must for pleasurable intercourse. If you want to enjoy your honeymoon, take some K-Y Jelly along with you. Use it liberally while you are caressing the genital area, particularly the very sensitive clitoral area.

Also, you will want to have a small towel within reach to take care of the discharged material (lubricating fluid mixed with semen) after ejaculation. We do not advise a vaginal douche after intercourse. The semen projected from the penis is primarily protein, similar to egg white, and is not dirty or unsanitary, despite its distinctive odor.

5. Agree in advance on your family-planning measures.

Fear of unwanted pregnancy can be a serious hindrance to sexual pleasure. Determine if you wish to use artificial means of family planning, natural means, or no means, and then make all necessary preparations in advance. You need to discuss this together and agree in advance on what measures, if any, should be taken. The responsibility belongs to both of you, and it should not cause uneasiness or uncertainty on your honeymoon.

You may find these statistics helpful. Studies have shown that 66 percent of pregnancies occur within three months of the initiation of unprotected intercourse. Within six months of continued exposure, 75 percent of the women have become pregnant, and by the end of one year about 80 percent of the women have conceived.

6. Make preparations for a painless first-time sexual experience.

At the time of their first intercourse, 50 percent of all women experience some pain; 20 percent say they have no pain; and 30 percent experience severe pain. The cause of this discomfort is the hymen—a shelf-like membrane that surrounds but does not cover the lower opening to the vagina. In some instances, a baby girl is born without a hymen so that its absence is not necessarily an indication of loss of virginity. In other cases, it is so tough and resistant that at the time of pelvic examination, a physician can predict that intercourse will be extremely uncomfortable for the bride.

The opening in the hymen for a virgin is usually about one inch, but for intercourse a diameter of one and one-half inches is needed. This means that the vaginal opening should be stretched in advance so that a painful tearing will not occur when the husband attempts to insert the penis. The physician can dilate the vagina if the patient requests; or the woman can devote a few moments each day for two to four weeks before the wedding in stretching the vaginal opening herself (the best way, in our opinion); or the bridegroom can be instructed in how to do it on the wedding night.

Here is how to stretch the vaginal opening. Begin by placing one finger, well-lubricated with K-Y Jelly, inside the vagina and push back very forcibly but very slowly. When you are able to insert one finger all the way to the base, then try to place two well-lubricated fingers into the vagina, press downward and backward with quite firm pressure.

If the husband is attempting to stretch the vaginal opening on the wedding night, he may then insert the tips of three fingers, arranged in a wedge shape, well-lubricated with K- Y Jelly. (His fingernails must be filed smooth and short.) Place the fingertips in the vaginal opening, then press down very firmly toward the back, but very slowly. This should take from fifteen to thirty minutes to accomplish, moving the fingers only about one-eighth inch at a time until all three fingers can be inserted to the base.

This procedure will result in the stretching and possibly even the tearing of small areas in the vaginal opening. If a small area of bleeding occurs, do not be afraid. Simply look for the exact spot that is bleeding, take a piece of tissue, put it on the spot and hold it there with a firm pressure. You will be able to stop whatever bleeding occurs in this manner. If another tear and more bleeding occurs when you have intercourse, you can stop it the same way by holding tissue on the exact spot with a firm pressure. The tissue may be left in placc about twelve hours and then soaked loose in warm water to avoid new bleeding. Intercourse can begin again the next day.

After this stretching process, the major portion of the remaining hymen lies in a crescent shape across the back of the vaginal opening. You should keep in mind that it is much less in the way when the wife's legs are down flat. If the husband has difficulty in accomplishing initial entrance, try this special position.

The bride lies on her back with two pillows under her hips, with her legs down as flat as possible to move the hymen more out of the way. The husband faces her and approaches from directly above so that the penis is in an almost vertical position at first contact. After applying plenty of K-Y Jelly around the vaginal opening and on the head of the penis, he places the tip of the penis near the front of the vaginal opening and slides it almost straight down, attempting to slip past the elastic hymen. When the penis slips into the vagina, then the wife should slowly and intermittently bring her knees up as far as her discomfort will permit. At this point the husband will no longer force the penis in but allow her to thrust her pelvis upward and forward against the partially inserted penis, which should still be an almost vertically straight down position.

As a last resort only, if there is a great deal of pain, Nupercainal Ointment may be applied around the vaginal opening, especially toward the back, and left for a period of five minutes. This is a local anesthetic ointment available without a prescription, which you may wish to have on hand if your physician has warned of a vaginal outlet that seems to be unusually tight.

While these precautions may sound unnecessary to many of you, pain on the wedding night does occur in some cases, and it can and often does affect the couple's sexual relationship for years to come. Some patients at the Wheat Clinic come to us after months or even years of avoiding sex because of a painful first experience. By the time they come to us, their marriage is hanging in the balance.

Most pain occurs from entering too quickly, not allowing enough time for the muscles around the vagina to relax. At the time of first intercourse, the husband should not strive to bring his wife to orgasm with his penis in the vagina. This will only increase her soreness and discomfort. After the penis is inserted, the husband should have his orgasm quickly, withdraw the penis, and gently stimulate his wife's clitoral area with his fingers to bring her to orgasm.

If the husband gives his wife tender loving care at this special time in her life, it will establish an attitude of trust within her so that in the weeks to come she can relax totally and enjoy his lovemaking.

Another problem may arise on your honeymoon unless plenty of lubrication is provided for the penis in the vagina. It is a bruising of the urethra, the outlet for urine from the bladder. (This opening is about one-half inch above the vaginal opening and entirely separate from it.) The urethra is a tube that runs beneath the pubic bone and can be easily bruised by the thrusting of the penis unless the penis and vagina are well-lubricated.

This bruising produces a bladder infection commonly called "honeymoon cystitis." It is characterized by pain in the bladder area and by blood in the urine with rather severe burning when the urine passes. The infection and pain will clear up more quickly if the bride increases her intake of fluids and uses medication prescribed by her physician.

Almost all urinary tract infections in women occur within forty-eight hours after sexual intercourse. Voiding within a few minutes after intercourse is important because bladder urine is sterile. Thus, the voiding of urine cleanses the urethral mechanism of bacteria which would cause the infection.

7. Do not be concerned about your lack of experience. We have never encountered a couple who had problems relating sexually because of their inexperience. In fact, some of the couples who enjoy the most fulfilling relationships came to us for premarriage counsel with no experience because they had chosen to wait until marriage. Their joy in one another was undiluted by past experiences, and they were free to discover what God has prepared in marriage for those who wait for His timing. What one needs for his wedding night is not experience, but correct information.

Now we want to direct our words to all couples, newlymarried or about to be.

SECRETS OF SEXUAL FULFILLMENT

If you are like most couples today, you are eager to experience every good thing; your expectations are high. If your sexual relationship falls short of total fulfillment, you will consider it a problem and search for the solution. The silent endurance and trial-and-error methods of your parents and grandparents are not for you! We consider this a positive development, for we know that satisfying sexual intimacy has a remarkable power to renew, refresh, and sustain a marriage.

In this section we want to give you seven valuable secrets of sexual fulfillment. Remember that secrets are things either concealed from others or not readily understood by them. Although sex seems to be the Western world's favorite topic with such exhaustive coverage by the media that we wonder if anything *could* still be concealed, the truth is that husbands and wives today are as frustrated as ever because of their inability to please one another sexually. But it doesn't have to be that way! Many troubled people come to the Wheat Clinic with problems in their sexual relationship that could have been avoided if only they had known and applied this counsel at the beginning of their marriage.

1. Forget the past.

"Like a lily among the thorns, so is my darling among the maidens " (Song of Sol. 2:2 NASV).

This is a key point today when so many people are going into a second marriage or may have had previous sexual experience outside of marriage. One mate may be tempted to make comparisons. Or the other mate may be tempted to be jealous and troubled by mental pictures of the lover loving someone else. Either condition may lead to great distress and a breakdown in the sexual relationship.

It is more difficult, at best, to establish the one flesh relationship when you have had sex before with another person or persons. So be forewarned that this is one area of life where experience will hinder rather than help. Here are the best ways to cope with prior sexual experience in a new marriage: Forget it and discipline yourself never to think of it or the person again; never, under any circumstances, discuss it with your partner. If it must be referred to, be careful never to give details—they will be particularly hard for your partner to forget. Do all you can to overcome its negative potential by practicing the art of loving your partner in all ways, not just sexually.

Learn from the bridegroom in the Song of Songs who wisely and lovingly reassured his bride that she was unique, his perfect one; that she was lovely as a lily and all other women were but as thorns in comparison.

Pray that God will enable you to forget your past sexual experience and make all things new for you in your marriage. It is easier to forget what lies behind when we are straining forward to what lies ahead and giving our heart and energies to that. So pour your life into loving your mate and give no emotional energy to things and persons of the past. God will be faithful to do His part: "... His compassions never fail. They are new every morning; great is your faithfulness" (Lam. 3:22–23).

2. Gain a lover's expertise.

"Let his left hand be under my head and his right hand embrace me" (Song of Sol. 2:6 NASV).

While it is true that a mastery of technique alone will do little for your love life, there are several things every husband needs to know to bring his wife to a satisfying sexual release.

(1) The clitoris is the trigger of female desire.

Men sometimes expect the greatest sexual sensitivity to be in the vagina, but this is not the case. The clitoris is the most keenly sensitive point for sexual arousal and has, as far as we know, no other function. Sufficient physical stimulation of the clitoral area will produce orgasm in nearly all women, if there has been sufficient foreplay and emotional arousal.

It's important to learn the exact location of the wife's clitoris. The clitoral shaft, which is about an inch long, is closed in by the peak of the inner lips, the labia minora, and extends upward onto the pelvic bone. At the outer end of the clitoris is the glans, a small rounded body about the size of a pea. A fold of skin, called the clitoral hood partly covers the glans.

During the time of sexual arousal when effective physical contact on the clitoris is continued, a firmness and enlargement of the shaft of the clitoris occurs. You can

detect this enlarged shaft by placing sensitive, well-lubricated fingertips alongside it. As you move your fingers
across the shaft from side to side, it will be like rolling your
fingers across a very small telephone cord. Persistent,
loving, gentle, sensitive, well-lubricated stimulation alongside this clitoral shaft will bring almost any wife to orgasm
in a twenty-minute period. As orgasm is approached, the
tempo of the stimulation will need to increase. Beware of
too much stimulation on the glans, as it can easily become
irritated. It is a super-sensitive spot! The wife should
lovingly move her husband's hand to show him which area
is most responsive to touch and even the degree of
stimulation and the tempo she prefers. This is part of
learning to communicate physically.

Remember, the clitoris must always be stimulated either
directly or indirectly for the wife to achieve orgasm. The
physical process of orgasm is the same whether by clitoral
stimulation or from sexual intercourse, which also stimu-
lates the clitoris through the movement of the penis as it
tugs and pulls at the small lips and the clitoral hood. Also,
certain positions will enable the base of the penis to rub
against the clitoris during intercourse and bring about
orgasm. When the woman experiences sexual release, she
will have a generalized sensation of pleasure throughout
the pelvis and especially at the vaginal opening. However,
the clitoris is always the trigger point of orgasm.

Men should also know that deep penetration of the
vagina has no effect on their wife's pleasure. The size of
the erect penis has almost nothing to do with how much
either partner enjoys intercourse, as only the outer two
inches of the vagina contain tissue that is stimulated by
pressure on the inside. Most vaginal sexual sensitivity
depends on contraction of the PC muscles as they grip the
penis, rather than being stretched by a larger object in the
vagina. In fact, during the plateau phase of arousal in
preparation for intercourse, the lower vagina swells so that

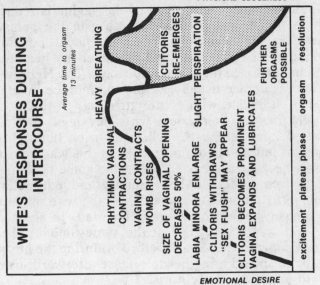

WIFE'S RESPONSES DURING INTERCOURSE

Average time to orgasm 13 minutes

PHYSICAL CLOSENESS

HEAVY BREATHING

CLITORIS RE-EMERGES

SLIGHT PERSPIRATION

RHYTHMIC VAGINAL CONTRACTIONS

VAGINA CONTRACTS

WOMB RISES

SIZE OF VAGINAL OPENING DECREASES 50%

LABIA MINORA ENLARGE

CLITORIS WITHDRAWS

"SEX FLUSH" MAY APPEAR

CLITORIS BECOMES PROMINENT

VAGINA EXPANDS AND LUBRICATES

FURTHER ORGASMS POSSIBLE

excitement   plateau phase   orgasm   resolution

EMOTIONAL DESIRE

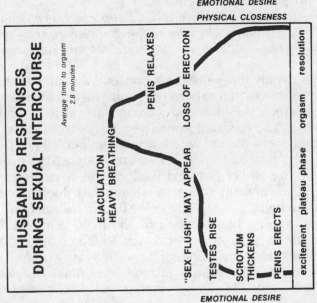

PHYSICAL CLOSENESS

HUSBAND'S RESPONSES DURING SEXUAL INTERCOURSE

Average time to orgasm 2.8 minutes

PENIS RELAXES

LOSS OF ERECTION

EJACULATION

HEAVY BREATHING

"SEX FLUSH" MAY APPEAR

TESTES RISE

SCROTUM THICKENS

PENIS ERECTS

excitement   plateau phase   orgasm   resolution

EMOTIONAL DESIRE

103

the diameter of the outer third of the vagina is reduced as much as 50 percent in readiness to grip the penis.

The Song of Songs describes the ideal position for stimulation. "Let his left hand be under my head and his right hand embrace me," the bride says. The Hebrew word translated embrace usually means to embrace lovingly, to fondle or stimulate with gentle stroking. In this position, the wife lies on her back with her legs comfortably separated, and her husband lies down on her right side, placing his left arm under her neck. In this way he can kiss her lips, neck, and breasts, and at the same time his right hand is free to fondle her genitals and particularly to stimulate the clitoris. In some cases, the wife may experience orgasm before the penis is inserted. In some cases, the two may reach orgasm at the same time. And, if the wife has not reached release before or during the husband's orgasm, he should bring her to release afterward, using his hand to stimulate the clitoris.

(2) After foreplay, the husband can reach orgasm in less than three minutes; the wife requires an average of thirteen minutes. The skillful lover understands and adjusts to this difference.

If you study these response charts, you will see the four phases of the sexual experience, and you can also take note of how much the man and woman vary in their timing of response. The husband must learn to control the timing of his response while the wife learns to let herself go, trusting both her husband and her own body. She needs to concentrate on her physical feelings and communicate her level of excitement to her husband with looks, touches, and sometimes loving words. While his stimulation brings on her orgasm, her caresses of the male genitalia do not speed up his orgasm. Instead, her touch of his genitals is soothing and comforting. The wife's very light, gentle caressing should center around the inner thighs, the scrotum, and the under surface of the penile shaft.

Fondling the head of the penis will increase his excitement and may trigger ejaculation more quickly than desired. By lovingly fondling her husband's genitals, the wife helps him to wait for her own excitement to build.

When is she ready for insertion of the penis? The most observable sign is the swelling of the inner lips on each side of the vaginal opening. These lips may be so engorged that they protrude beyond the outer lips. The wife should signal her husband when she desires the insertion of the penis, and it is best in most cases for the wife to insert it. Never thrust vigorously as soon as the penis is inserted, since this usually decreases arousal in the woman.

Timing is all-important. Take time to arouse each other completely. Take time to ensure her orgasm and his controlled, full response. And after intercourse, take time to express your love and appreciation to each other. The final phase has been called afterglow when the fires of passion and pleasure settle down to a warm, lovely glow. The couple should lie close in each other's arms, enjoy each other's presence, and show tenderness and appreciation with hugs, kisses, love pats, and loving words. This will give a smooth transition to complete relaxation. It may be as long as fifteen minutes before all the physical signs of arousal are gone. A young man's erection may remain as long as half an hour.

Some have wondered why God made men and women so different in length of time required for their sexual arousal. Here is Dr. Wheat's answer:

> If men and women both were satisfied with a short period of arousal, the sex act would become a brief, mechanical experience. If both took a very long time to become aroused, the experience could become boring and monotonous. . . . Because men and women are different, the husband is given the opportunity to learn self-control and encouraged to investigate and employ the imaginative techniques that please a woman. He has the opportunity to

105

develop patience and gentleness in physical communication, while she learns to keep him sexually aroused and intrigued. The differences between men and women provide ground for creative, interesting interaction and enrich the sexual relationship in marriage.[6]

3. Nourish your total relationship.

"Take us the foxes, the little foxes, that spoil the vines; for our vines have tender grapes" (Song of Sol. 2:15).

Sex in marriage serves, in sometimes uncomfortable ways, as a mirror of your total relationship, reflecting the flaws as well as the virtues. You might think of it as a barometer, which fluctuates, depending on how well you are getting along in other areas of your marriage. Negative feelings will often show up first in your sex life.

When people come to us, complaining of difficulties in relating sexually, we usually find that the difficulty began elsewhere and long before. Any unresolved conflict, sooner or later, finds its way into the bedroom where it creates a whole new set of problems. For instance, most of the cases we see of inhibited sexual desire have one root cause: repressed anger and resentment, which produce depression and a chilly indifference toward the mate.

Women are particularly sensitive to factors outside the bedroom. Dr. Helen Kaplan warns that "in general, female sexual desire is more variable than that of males. While women have a greater orgastic potential, their sexuality is also more easily suppressed."[7]

Researchers have found a strong connection between a woman's ability to reach an orgasm and her feelings of trust in her partner. If other problems in the marriage have caused her to question whether she can rely on her husband, it will make a difference in her sexual response. If she is insecure because she does not experience his cherishing, she may not be able to gain sexual release. Since she feels she can't depend on him and has to stand on her own, she finds it almost impossible to trust him in the sexual act and to relax and let herself go to the point of orgasm.

The sex drive of young men is so intense that only strongly negative factors will inhibit their desire. But a man's sexual life is always tied to his sense of manhood and self-esteem. If his wife consistently tears him down and demonstrates her lack of respect for him, over a period of time it will hinder his ability to desire sex or enjoy it. He may even have problems in functioning sexually with his wife.

These are three examples of a principle to remember: The way you treat your partner on a daily basis will determine your partner's responsiveness in the bedroom. On the positive side, this means that good sex at night begins in the morning in the way you snuggle together before getting up for work, the way you talk to each other over breakfast, the way you kiss good-by with a promise for the time when you can be together again. Any intimacy between you has sexual dimensions whether you're talking together or tossing a frisbee, dressing together for the day or working in the garden side by side, cooking dinner together or sharing a time of prayer. It's all a part of lovemaking.

We encourage you to nurture that relationship with particular attention in these areas:

(1) *Avoid behavior which creates anger and lasting resentment in your partner.* Try to resolve conflicts when they arise and do not let them drag on without getting help from your pastor or a biblical counselor.

(2) *Husband, demonstrate to your wife in every way you can that you won't let her down, that she's safe in the security of your love and permanent commitment.* Be the leader she can lean on and count on. Prove to her that you care about every detail of her welfare. This really can make the difference in her ability to respond to you fully.

(3) *Wife, remember that when your husband's self-esteem is reduced because he feels you do not respect him, your sex life together is sure to suffer.* Respecting your husband and responding to him as the leader in your home will inspire him to be the confident and ardent lover you want him to be.

(4) *Learn to relate as lovers all of the time, not just when having sex.* Feeling mutually loved and admired will keep you turned on sexually. As Dr. Kaplan says, "Love is the best aphrodisiac discovered so far."[8]

(5) *Pray that God will make you sensitive to areas of your relationship that are being neglected.* (Husbands tend to see their sex relationship separately from these areas, while wives never do.)

With proper care given to your total relationship, your sex life can be a joyful affirmation of the love you share twenty-four hours a day.

4. Keep negatives out of your lovemaking.

"You are altogether beautiful, my darling, and there is no blemish in you" (Song of Sol. 4:7 NASV).

Students of human behavior tell us that all human behavior is organized around seeking pleasure and avoiding pain. Apply this to your sexual relationship. You can see how important it is to keep negatives out of the bedroom and to make your lovemaking altogether pleasurable.

You need to look on sex in your marriage as an opportunity for genuine "lovemaking" in the sense of making or building love. This will happen through giving and receiving in ways that are physically and emotionally satisfying for both of you. Remember, the thrills are great, but concentrate on the essentials: physical/emotional closeness and a positive response that will signal pleasure, not the emotional pain of rejection and criticism.

Compare the generous, positive words of the husband in the Song of Songs ("Thou art all fair, my love; there is no spot in thee.") with these examples taken from real life. A husband complains,

"Elizabeth's idea of foreplay is a brief therapy session, which consists mostly of criticism of me. That's supposed to be how we get intimate. Usually, though, it ends in our sleeping reverse spoons."9

A wife confides,

"My sex life has become a nightmare because my husband is a dictator in the bedroom. George is always trying to control our lovemaking and wants things his own way without any regard for what I prefer or can do. Now he insists that we reach orgasm simultaneously! I'd like to just forget the whole thing."

A husband says,

I can't believe the way Jill treats me when we're making love. She starts complaining about my technique instead of just showing me what she wants. Or she cracks jokes—jokes that put me down. It hurts.

A wife asks,

"How can I break my husband away from the eleven o'clock news to go to bed? I get up at 5:30 a.m., so by the time Tom is ready to make love, I'm wiped out. His selfishness really hurts me, and it's affecting our entire marriage."

Therapists call negative behavior that hinders a satisfying sexual experience "sexual sabotage." The behavior that creates the deepest resentment of all in wives is the feeling that they are being used, not loved. For instance, a man may feel desire and want sex even when he is angry with his partner. That's the last thing a hostile wife wants. She feels exploited and outraged by his attempts to have sex before their relationship has been put right. The behavior that offends a husband is the critiquing of his performance or, worst of all, a lack of response from his wife, which amounts to rejection.

It's good to follow the biblical principle in your bedroom: "If there be any virtue, and if there be any praise, think on these things" (Phil. 4:8 b). The Greek word for think is an accounting term that means reckon these things among your assets. If you are positive in your attitude and your approach, your sexual relationship can mirror a love that values, treasures, and respects.

5. Practice bedroom etiquette.

". . . it is the voice of my beloved that knocketh, saying, Open to me, my sister, my love . . ." (Song of Sol. 5:2).

Here is one of the memorable letters to advice columnist Abigail Van Buren and her even more memorable answer:

Dear Abby: What would you do with a man who refuses to use a deodorant, seldom bathes, and doesn't even own a toothbrush? —Stinky's Wife.

Dear Wife: Absolutely nothing![10]

To approach your partner without being clean and well-groomed is simply bad manners. When married, bathing at night before getting into bed makes sense. Sleeping together, even when not making love, is an intimate contact. When you want to make love, bathing, shaving, and carefully grooming yourself shows respect as well as caring and an anticipation of closeness.

Have you ever thought of applying all you know about good manners and courtesy in your times of relating sexually? The purpose of etiquette is to smooth and improve human relations. Many sexual problems result from ignoring bedroom etiquette, and good manners in the sexual relationship could cure some of the dysfunctions we must treat.

The truly courteous are warm, kind, generous, and flexible in the bedroom. They consider one another's needs and feelings, and approach sex with their partner not as a right, but a privilege. Courtesy is made up of tact and foresight—looking ahead to see how what you say or do will affect another person. Tact means to touch delicately. As a considerate lover, you will try to relate to your loved one with this "delicacy of touch," and you will avoid being careless or rude in the name of relaxed intimacy.

6. Share the responsibility.

"I am my beloved's, and my beloved is mine. . ." (Song of Sol. 6:3).

Sexual fulfillment requires a sharing of the responsibility for every aspect of the relationship. Both of you are responsible to communicate (lovingly!) your needs and desires—the ways of loving that please you most. You're also responsible to communicate (tactfully!) what you don't care for by suggesting something else in its place.

Sexual communication is important, but so is taking partial responsibility for your own sexual arousal and satisfaction. The wife should realize that her mind is probably the most important part of her sexual anatomy, and that she needs to prepare herself ahead of time for pleasure, fantasizing romantically about her husband and anticipating the experience. She must learn to use her own mental concentration to sustain the emotional mood of lovemaking and then guide her husband in the kind of physical stimulation she desires for orgasm. She also is responsible to initiate sex when she desires it.

The husband can learn to do what will increase the physical intensity and pleasure of his orgasm: (1) waiting at least twenty-four hours after orgasm to allow the body to store a larger volume of seminal fluid; (2) lengthening the foreplay and excitement periods so that the penis can remain erect about twenty minutes; (3) concentrating on enjoyment of the wife's response; (4) voluntarily contracting the anal sphincter muscles during orgasm; and (5) increasing the force of thrusting while the orgasm is in progress.

If a problem arises in your sexual relationship, you need to take responsibility for it together. It is a couple problem that will require a couple solution, so absolutely refrain from placing blame on one another. Remember that every sexual problem has a solution that can lead to pleasure and emotional satisfaction for both partners. For a full discussion of common sexual problems and what to do about them, we refer you to *Intended for Pleasure*, which will answer your questions.

Remember also that you share the responsibility with God, the Wedding Guest in the Song of Songs, who encouraged the lovers to delight in the sexual relationship He had designed for them. Make your relationship a matter of prayer. When problems arise, it may be necessary to go to a physician or therapist. But the solution also requires

patience and purity of love, and a sincere turning toward God. If a couple were to seek the Lord with their whole will, rejoice in Christian fellowship, and spend time both alone and together in heartfelt prayer and study of the Scriptures, they would soon find their love life filled with a rich glow and a mysterious new energy that cannot be discovered through any worldly means. For as the Lord is the author of sex, so He is its interpreter, and it is His therapy that is most to be treasured.[11]

7. Enjoy partner-centered sex.

"The mandrakes give fragrance, and at our gates are all manner of pleasant fruits, new and old, which I have laid up for thee, O my beloved" (Song of Sol. 7:13).

This is the greatest secret of sexual fulfillment we can offer you: to develop a relationship that is not self-centered, not performance-centered, not even sex-centered, but centered in the joy of giving your partner pleasure. In this best kind of sexual relationship, each learns how to please the other; each tries to outdo the other in pleasing; and each gets the greatest thrills from seeing the other's ecstatic response.

When two people enjoy partner-centered sex, their lovemaking is never repetitious, boring, or mechanical. Sex that has become as routine as brushing teeth or as mechanical as mailing a letter signals a dying relationship. It can be revived when both put the focus on their partner's pleasure. The signs of life are spontaneity and sensitivity to one another.

Partner-centered sex depends on your motivation, for it will require careful study of your partner to learn what brings pleasure (and displeasure) to him or her. Becoming sensitive to your partner's needs and desires, implied or stated, means listening with your whole being to that person. It involves reading body language, observing even the slightest word or gesture and discerning what it means. You will lovingly put forth effort to discover your partner's wishes, to find out what "feels good." You will learn your partner's likes, dislikes, what parts of his or her body are most erotic, and the ways of loving that evoke a response at that particular moment.

All of this requires the gift of time to one another and the decision to set your marriage bed apart as an important priority. Knowing that simple exhaustion because of hard work, a demanding schedule, small children, or too much social life will diminish sexual interest, the two of you need to establish a lifestyle that avoids fatigue and saves prime time and energy for one another.

Don't think of partner-centered sex as somehow sacrificial. You don't lose any pleasure by this. To concentrate on pleasuring your partner is a sweet sacrifice that turns out to be no sacrifice at all because the reward is so great! The thrills that come to both of you as you each see your partner responding totally and enjoying your lovemaking cannot be described.

Partner-centered sex will be positive, relaxed, enjoyable, romantic, physically satisfying, and emotionally fulfilling. Partner-centered sex partners will learn to handle their relationship with the care that they would give to anything that can be explosively wonderful, or explosively harmful if mishandled. Yes, there is a risk in being vulnerable. But the same openness that makes you vulnerable to pain is the price of joy. More than that, it is the prerequisite for oneness.

Sexual fulfillment that bonds the two of you in the forever relationship of marriage will include these elements: the assurance of being accepted and desired; the well-being that comes from intimate physical and emotional closeness; the sensuous delights of loving caresses; and the wonderful feeling of belonging to each other in the one-flesh relationship of God's devising.

7

The ABCs of Never: Warning Signals

In this day of "instant" everything, when experts are asked to sum up their solution to a pressing world problem "in the fifteen seconds we have left," we offer some almost-instant counsel for your new marriage.

You've read the ABCs of Forever. Here is another set of ABCs, but these form the language of loss, not love: loss of happiness, loss of peace, loss of all good things you hoped to get from your marriage. It's said that most people marry for sex, security, and prevention of loneliness. Turning these ABCs loose in your marriage will destroy your joy in sex and your sense of emotional security; moreover, if allowed to proceed unchecked, they can produce more loneliness in your relationship than you ever felt when you walked this world as a single.

We call thse the *ABCs of Never* because they can never bring you happiness. But understanding them, avoiding them, and replacing them with positive attitudes and hehavior will go far to guard your love relationship and increase your pleasure in it.

These "ABCs" have their model in the Proverbs of the Old Testament, a book which sets forth a series of momentous rules of life, concentrated into remarkably few words. Although ours offer more words and less genius, they are grounded in biblical truth. They should serve as warning signs and reference points when you feel your relationship is moving in the wrong direction.

Adultery

Sexual intercourse with someone other than your marriage partner.

One of the deadly three destroyers in marriage, it shocks the heart and destroys the lifeline of trust, but does not release you from the vows of marriage. Only marriage to someone else destroys the marriage bond. Even when a Christian marriage is attacked by unfaithfulness, it can be restored and healed. God says adultery carries severe penalties with it. Read Proverbs 5 and 1 Corinthians 6:9–20.

Anger

Uncontrolled or unresolved feelings of hostility expressed through temper tantrums, hurtful words, pouting, or icy rages during which you refuse to acknowledge the other's presence.

Uncontrolled, unresolved anger destroys love and produces bitterness and depression. It's an ineffectual way of resolving differences. Never go to bed when angry, i.e., never let a quarrel continue on the second day. Stay up and talk, stay up and pray. Resolve it, and go to sleep with your closeness restored. Proverbs 17:14 says a quarrel begins like a small hole in a reservoir, letting out a tiny trickle. But if it is not stopped, the hole is enlarged and a destructive flood pours through. The problem is not the anger itself, but failure to handle it biblically and resolve it with mutual forgiveness. Read Ephesians 4 and 5.

Bitterness

Anger pushed inward until it takes root, producing all manner of trouble and grief including damage to your physical health.

This second deadly destroyer of marriage comes from clinging to an unforgiving spirit. It tortures both you and your partner, ravaging secretly while blocking any attempts to build real intimacy. Because it operates beneath the surface, it may not be recognized until almost too late. Bitterness can be removed only through forgiveness which Jesus Christ makes possible, "To forgive is to set a prisoner free and discover that the prisoner was you." Read Hebrews 12:12–15; Ephesians 4:31; and Colossians 3:19.

Change

What you can't make your partner do, and it would be better never to try.

You can never change another person's behavior, but you can set up the conditions whereby that person motivates himself (or herself) to change—and to seek the Lord's enabling power in changing. Never forget the positive effects of unconditional acceptance. Read Romans 5 and 6. Also the Song of Solomon.

Conflict

An inevitable happening when two are learning to share their life, but when mishandled, conflicts can escalate and lead to disaster for the marriage.

Basically, there are four ways of handling a marital conflict: 1) The *chaos* principle when husband and wife clash by day and night and fight incessantly, or quit trying and go their own ways. As a result, anarchy reigns in the home. 2) The *power play* principle where one eventually "wins" and the other "loses." In a power play, the entire offense converges at a given point to exert mass pressure on the defense. When this happens in a marriage, both lose. One dominates, the other retaliates with passive-aggressive behavior or deep resentments. 3) The *bargain-*

ing table principle where conflicts are solved by the *quid pro quo* method (something in return). This is preferable to chaos, but depends on a selfish assertion of one's rights, although done in a civilized manner. 4) The *grace* principle which can be understood and implemented only by Christians. It is modeled after God's gracious treatment of us in Jesus Christ which gives freely and does not think in terms of bargains and rights. Grace means to bestow gracious favors unconditionally. Read Ephesians 2:4–9 and Romans 6:14.

Criticism

A bad habit of forming and expressing negative opinions concerning your partner's appearance, behavior, personality, and choices in life.

It may seem fairly harmless, even "constructive" under certain circumstances. Yet it has the potential to bring about the slow, painful death of a love relationship: when criticism drips unchecked, love dies by inches. The third deadly destroyer of marriage, criticism should be replaced by encouragement and edifying. Read 1 Peter 4:8; Romans 14:19, 15:2; 1 Thessalonians 5:11; and 1 Corinthians 8:1.

Debt

The habit of spending more than your income, relying on loans and credit cards, and hoping to make enough in the future to pay for what you are using today.

Two principles can avert the disasters of this approach: Decide you won't spend what you don't have; and trust God to provide for your needs instead of trusting loans. Overwhelming financial pressures are a key factor in the majority of divorces today. Obtain personal financial counsel and develop a biblical approach to money and possessions. When both partners must work, here are some suggested guidelines:

1. Arrange to have your time off at the same time.
2. Live as close to work as possible; eliminate travel time.
3. Try to get jobs in the same area of town.
4. Recognize that the extra money isn't worth it if you're never together.
5. Discuss your work with one another.
6. Respect one another's skills and hard work.
7. Don't make your partner jealous.
8. Plan ahead financially for the time when the wife will want to be home as you begin your family.
9. Avoid consumer debt and multiply your choices.

Read Psalm 112:5; Proverbs 3:5–10, 15:16, 16:8; Matthew 6:19-34; Luke 12:15–21; 2 Corinthians 9:6-15; Philippians 4:19; and 1 Timothy 6:6–11.

Disloyalty

The harmful practice of criticizing your partner in discussions with friends and relatives, or allowing them to criticize your mate.

The words you speak—or hear—have power to reinforce negative thoughts and influence your attitude against the person with whom you are meant to be *one* in body, mind, heart, and spirit. D. James Kennedy, in his book *Learning to Live with the People You Love,* points out that marriage can be either tremendously constructive or unimaginably destructive to the lives of those involved. What makes the difference? Whether you are building each other up or tearing one another down! Read Mark 10:6-9 and 1 Corinthians 13:7.

Ego Trips

Making yourself look "good" at the expense of your partner's feelings.

This is done by cutting your mate down, humiliating him

119

or her publicly, or indulging in misplaced humor which ridicules your partner. People with low self-images sometimes resort to this unpleasant behavior to build themselves up. Read Ephesians 5:28; Proverbs 31:11, 26; Colossians 3:8; Ephesians 4:29 and 5:4.

Failure to Communicate

Choosing (for whatever reason) to shut the door of your heart and soul, leaving your loved one "on the outside, looking in."

It's most important to seek the help of a biblical counselor to remedy this, for the causes are varied and complex. Read 1 Thessalonians 2:8; John 15:15; and Romans 1:12.

Guilt Trips

Making your partner feel guilty.

Guilt statements, such as "I'm very disappointed in you," quench feelings of love and pleasure in being together. Guilt is a most disagreeable feeling which people prefer to avoid. Remember, the Holy Spirit has the sole responsibility of convicting of sin in a way that brings about healing and redemption. Only the Word of God can effectively reprove, correct, and train us in the way we should go. Read John 16:7-8, 13; and 11 Timothy 3:16-17.

Habits

Habitual practices that are injurious to your health and happiness: anything which alters the thinking part of the mind, distorts the emotions, harms the body, or leads to harmful acts, such as cocaine, marijuana, and all other forms of illegal drugs; misuse of prescription drugs; beverage alcohol ("drinking"); smoking; and eating disorders.

What hurts you hurts your partner too. But God can

deliver you! Commit your way to Him and seek help from your pastor, your physician, your biblical counselor, or support groups that may be of benefit. Read Proverbs 20:1; 23:29–35; Galatians 5:16–25; 6:8; 1 Corinthians 10:13; and Romans 13:13–14.

Impatience

Annoyance at having to tolerate any delay or general irritability expressed in quick, sharp retorts and a "hurry-up" attitude.

This is hard to live with! However, an impatient person can learn to be quiet, steady, and even-tempered, if he or she desires to change. If we allow Him to, the Lord works mighty changes in us. Read Proverbs 17:27; Galatians 5:22; and James 1:2–4 with Psalm 62:5.

Indifference

A lack of response to your partner, sending the message that you really don't care.

This form of unlove can have the most serious consequences, because all the loves of marriage, with the exception of *agape,* require a response to keep them alive. Indifference, rather than hatred, is the opposite of love. Read Song of Solomon and 1 Peter 1:22.

Inequality

An unfair load of responsibility placed on one partner for the necessities of maintaining their shared life.

This includes financial burdens; housekeeping and home maintenance; duties toward parents and children; and the daily tasks and errands which must be done. Neither partner should be allowed to assume all of this, and neither should be expected to carry it. Inequities produce weariness and resentments. Read Proverbs 18:9; Ecclesiastes

4:9, 9:9–10; Matthew 11:28–30; Galatians 6:2; and Colossians 3:23–24.

Insensitivity

Deafness and blindness of the heart toward your partner's feelings and needs.

This is like trampling with clodhopper boots over the other person—not out of malice, but ignorance. Love pays the most careful attention to the beloved. Anyone can learn to be sensitive to another person. Read 1 Peter 3:7–8, Romans 12:15, and Song of Solomon. Also, the Letter of Paul to Philemon as a model of sensitivity to another person in a delicate situation.

Jealousy

An inordinate fear of losing your partner that causes you to behave irrationally.

This is a destroyer which feeds on your own insecurities and suspicions, and makes your partner miserable. But neither should behave in ways to inspire suspicions. Particularly avoid paying undue attention by look, comment, or time spent with another person of the opposite sex. Never give your partner cause to feel ignored, unappreciated, or threatened by your admiration for someone else. Read Song of Solomon 8:6.

"Keeping House" Controversies

Arguments, strong differences of opinion over the way to do things in your shared home.

Disagreements over the toothpaste tube or the best way to rinse dishes may sound like minor difficulties, but this sort of friction in your household affairs can become a source of great frustration. Compromise, tolerance, a sense of humor, and a sense of proportion can carry you through this problem until you have learned to adapt yourselves to one another. Read Romans 12:9–11 with Galatians 5:22.

Lack of Intimacy

A superficial relationship which leaves a dangerous emotional void in your marriage.

Intimacy will cause you to stay in love. Without intimacy one or both may be strongly tempted to seek it elsewhere. Human beings have an insatiable desire for a meaningful one-to-one relationship. Read Song of Solomon 2:3–6; 14.

Messiness

Disorder in the management and arrangement of your possessions which creates havoc in your household.

A comfortable, orderly home which offers a peaceful atmosphere makes for marital happiness. Creative clutter is one thing; messiness which drives your partner (and you, too) "up the wall" needs to be remedied. God, truly, is the God of order, not of confusion. Many fine "help" books are available to take you through this problem. When one determines to keep a *perfect* house, that also can cause discomfort and unhappiness. Your goal should be: a home you both can enjoy and the freedom to invite people into your house without worrying about its "disaster area" appearance. Read 1 Corinthians 14:33; Proverbs 31:27; and Hebrews 13:1–2.

Nagging

Tormenting your partner by complaining constantly to get your own way about something.

With this approach you admit your failure to deal with issues constructively, or to inspire your partner to love you. But nagging never improves the situation, and may be the death blow to love and intimacy. Instead of nagging, apply the potent power of praise. Read Proverbs 12:25, 15:15, 17:1, 25:23–24; Galatians 5:15, 26; Colossians 3:12–17; and Hebrews 10:24.

Out-of-Control Children

The disruptive presence of unruly, undisciplined children.

It is hard to build a meaningful love relationship when your children are out of control. If their misbehavior and unreasonable demands give you no time for intimacy and private enjoyment of one another, it's imperative to deal with the situation. If you're beginning a family, establish the patterns of obedience in their earliest training. Help them to understand that they must respect your privacy and your right to a peaceful, well-ordered home. It will be a blessing both to your children and your marriage. Read 1 Timothy 3:4; Ephesians 6:1–4; and God's principles of disciplining His children: Hebrews 12:5–11 with Proverbs 3:11–12.

Parental Pressures

Interference from your families, in-law strife, family "feuds," or too much closeness to your parents, and dependence on them.

The biblical principle is: Leave your parents and cleave to your marriage partner; establish a new family unit. You are no longer responsible to obey your parents, but you are responsible to honor them and care for them when they need it. Your families, by their influence and example and the respect they show for your new marriage and your mate, can be of great help to you. Unfortunately, some families become a great hindrance. Read Genesis 2:24; Ephesians 6:1–3; 1 Timothy 5:8.

Pride

The thing which keeps you from seeking forgiveness or granting it.

This character trait is most displeasing to God. It's also one of the highest barriers to a loving relationship. In a good give-and-take marriage, both partners recognize their own shortcomings and willingly admit their flaws. When you learn to say things like, "I was wrong . . . I'm sorry. . . . I need you, . . . " you're on your way to overcoming the pride that destroys marriages. Read Proverbs 6:17, 13:10, 21:4; Romans 12:3, 16; and James 5:16.

Procrastination

When your failure to do what should be done when it should be done creates frustrations in your marriage partner and unhappiness for yourself.

Putting off until later what you have time for today becomes a terrible form of indebtedness, and can be a great annoyance to your marriage partner. The Bible calls the classic procrastinator a *sluggard* who will not begin things; or will not finish things, once started; or will not face things that need to be dealt with. Read Proverbs 6:6–11, 10:26, 12:24–27, 13:4, 15:19, 18:9, 19:24, 20:4, 21:25–26; 22:13, 24:30–32, and 26:15–16.

Quick Replies

Sins of the tongue which come from speaking before you think.

Sharp answers and cutting responses fall under the category of verbal abuse. This creates a strong desire to avoid the person who's causing the pain. Be warned that, in time, it can drive your partner away from you. Read Psalm 19:14, 141:3; Proverbs 12:18, 15:1, 19:11, 29:20; and James 3:5–12.

Rejection, Sexual

Defrauding your partner by refusing sex.

This creates intense grief and loss of self-respect for the rejected partner. When sex becomes a part of the battleground of marriage, or when either devalues sex, both partners have lost something very important. The sexual relationship in marriage is meant to be one of the most mysterious, profound, and enriching of all experiences. God gives clear-cut guidelines in the Scriptures concerning sexual responsibilities in marriage. Read Proverbs 5:18 and 1 Corinthians 7:2–5.

Selfishness

Preoccupation with yourself, putting your well-being before your marriage partner's.

This indicates that you have not yet learned how to love. Love is giving without counting the cost because it is unimportant compared with the joy of serving the beloved. Read John 3:16; Philippians 2:3–8; and 2 Corinthians 12:15; with Mark 14:1–9.

Self-pity

Feeling sorry for yourself and expressing it by whining and complaining.

This is so tiresome for the partner who must listen to it continually. Replace negative feelings with prayer and thanksgiving. Read Philippians 2:14; 4:6–7; and 1 Thessalonians 5:18.

Spiritual Indifference

In essence, a refusal to recognize God as God; a denial of the Lordship of Jesus Christ in your life even though you may consider yourself a Christian, saved by His grace.

The symptoms are a lack of interest in Bible reading, prayer, and church attendance. You are robbing yourself, your mate, and your family of God's blessing. One of the best ways to ensure a lasting marriage is to become active members of a Bible-teaching church. For example: Two economists studied 1,800 families for twelve years. They found that no-fault divorce laws, educational achievements, and the employment of the wives had little effect on whether couples divorced. But one thing did matter: *The risk of divorce was higher for couples who did not attend church regularly!* Read Deuteronomy 5:29, 6: 4–7; Joshua 1:8, 24:14–15; Galatians 6:7–10; 1 Timothy 3:15; 11 Timothy 3:14–17; and Hebrews 10:25.

Television

The over-use of television until it becomes harmful to your relationship.

Too much TV-watching produces passive people with neither the motivation nor energy to develop intimate marriages. It can be a serious hindrance to your sex life and communication. Read 1 Corinthians 10:23 with Ecclesiastes 2:10–11.

Ultimatums

The *or else* weapon which people use to try to make their marriage partner change.

This usually involves the threat of divorce; it is unbiblical and *very* unwise. Divorce should not remain in the vocabulary of a couple who want a love-filled, lasting marriage. Keeping divorce as an escape clause indicates a flaw in your commitment to each other which can prove to be fatal. Threats are always nonproductive and often backfire. Read Malachi 2:14-16; Mark 10:1-9; and 1 Peter 3:8–9.

Violence

Physical expressions of rage resulting from anger out of control.

This more frequently involves abusing objects rather than people, i.e., throwing things. It is a sign of immaturity which can be overcome by learning effective techniques for dealing with your feelings. The expression of violence toward loved ones is totally unacceptable behavior and has no place in your marriage. If even one instance occurs, seek help from a biblical counselor immediately. Read Genesis 6:11; Proverbs 4:14–17; and 11 Peter 1:3–7.

Withholding Affection

Refusing to give your marriage partner the loving, affectionate, nonsexual physical touching that he or she needs.

A tender touch tells us we are cared for; it can calm our fears, soothe our pain, comfort our hearts, and grant us emotional security. To refuse to touch your partner lovingly sends the opposite message and may send your partner searching for love elsewhere. Read the Song of Solomon and Ecclesiastes 4:11 with the principle of meeting need from 1 John 3:17–18.)

Xhaustion

An absence of the vitality you need for your marriage because you are so involved in other areas of life that you have little left to give to your partner and your love relationship.

Work together to resolve this problem. Few things in life are as important as your marriage, and it does take energy to maintain a good relationship. Read Psalm 116:7; 11 Thessalonians 3:16; and Song of Solomon 5:2–8.

Yelling and Other Annoying Habits

Any personal habit which gets on your partner's nerves.

For example, he yells and she "can't stand it." She "pops" her chewing gum, and it sends him out of the room. Marriage puts every problem and even the smallest annoyance under a magnifying glass because it's so *daily*. We have to learn to be both tolerant of habits that bother us and sensitive to our partner's wishes in trying not to offend. (After all, when we love someone, we don't want to make that person unhappy!) This problem takes time to work through and a good supply of patience and self-control. Love will work a change if we let it have its way instead of forcing the issue through nagging, criticizing, and asserting our rights. Read 1 Corinthians 13:7.

Zzz's

Boredom with your partner, your marriage, and your life in general.

Boredom is a tragic waste of the gift of life, and an insult to your partner. Bored people are boring people. Bored people become depressed people. So take action to change your attitude, put the spark back in your marriage, and find joy and excitement in knowing God and discovering how He wants you to serve Him. Read Psalm 36:7–9; Psalm 118:24; Proverbs 4:18; and Philippians 1:21.

THE MOST DANGEROUS YEARS

We are often asked what are the most stressful years in a marriage. They include these times:

The first two years of adjustment and adaptation

The sixth and seventh years when outside temptations are said to be the greatest

The period when the "honeymoon" phase is over and each may begin to view the other separately and critically

Any time when one or both feel bored with their relationship because it is not vital and growing

The middle years when children leave home and partners must once again depend on one another for their companionship and love

Any time when people have the financial freedom and the opportunity to be unfaithful if they choose

The hard times when outside pressures and problems become acute, particularly in the areas of employment and finances or grief and loss

Periods of physical illness and enforced separation, for various reasons

Old age, when people may have less control over their privacy and their circumstances.

At any age or stage, you should be most careful to guard your oneness and never let other people—whether it be children, parents, siblings, co-workers, or friends—intrude into your own private world of love. They have their place in your life, but it is never at the center of your relationship.

How to Love Your Wife: The Husband's Handbook

This chapter is for husbands, but we suspect it will be read with great interest by wives. Wives often tell us their husbands do not know how to love them, and men admit that it's a fact. Said one husband to us: "Meet her needs? I didn't even know that she had any special needs when we married. She liked me well enough when we dated, but it was a new game after the wedding, and I obviously didn't know the rules. I've been playing catch-up ever since!"

One observer has suggested that marriages fail because

all too often, people marry before acquiring the knowledge and skills necessary to take care of their mates: to meet their emotional, mental, and physical needs. One of the ironies in our society is that a person has to have four years of training to receive a plumber's license, but absolutely no training is required for a marriage license. Our educational system doesn't even require communication courses basic to the meaningful development of any relationship. As a result, many men and women enter marriage with virtually no knowledge of how to meet the basic emotional and mental needs of their mates.[1]

Fortunately, God has not left husbands helpless, nor dependent upon our educational system. God holds the answers for those who want, and even long, to love their wives—answers that are spelled out, written with clarity and power, and made as available to us as the nearest Bible. The "love adventure" really begins when we turn to the Scriptures to find out what the Creator recommends for our marriage.

In the next few pages we want to give you, in brief, the biblical counsel that can transform your relationship over a period of years, as you learn to love your wife in the ways her Creator advises. He knows what she needs. You may not, at this point. But He does!

Because He is God, He speaks by commandment and teaches by example. All the knowledge He provides for us on the subject can be compressed into this one imperative which depends upon a luminous example for its force: "Husbands, love your wives, even as Christ also loved the church, and gave himself for it" (Ephes. 5:25).

Your wife needs to be *loved*. But loved how? What will be required of you? To love her responsibly, understandingly, constructively, cherishingly, romantically, realistically, and (as the springboard from which the other loves rebound) sacrificially. When you have learned to do this, you will have loved her according to the commandment: ". . . even as Christ loved the church and gave himself for it."

Now let's take a closer look at each of these ways of meeting your wife's deepest needs.

1. LOVE HER WITH A RESPONSIBLE LOVE

Love your wife by taking responsibility for her. When couples develop marital problems and seek counseling with Dr. Wheat, he often tells the husband, "It might not be your fault, but that does not matter. It is always your responsibility."

Why do we start with this bare fact? Doesn't it sound

rather cold and hard? What does this have to do with the passionate love you *feel* for the woman you have married? Our answer is *everything*. Passion, romantic adoration, delight, liking, deep friendship—-all of this counts for very little in marriage without the husband's acceptance of the basic charge God has given him. Consider this carefully:

> Husband, love your wives, even as Christ also loved the church, and gave himself for it; That he might sanctify and cleanse it with the washing of water by the word, That he might present it to himself a glorious church, not having spot, or wrinkle, or any such thing; but that it should be holy and without blemish. So ought men to love their wives as their own bodies. He that loveth his wife loveth himself. For no man ever yet hated his own flesh; but nourisheth and cherisheth it, even as the Lord the church. . . . let every one of you in particular so love his wife even as himself (Ephes. 5:25–29, 33).

Think back to the beginning of your courting relationship. When did you first realize that you really loved this girl in particular? You will find that at that point you were beginning to take responsibility for her—that you had an active concern about her physical and emotional well-being and, indeed, everything that concerned her. Whether she was preparing for a chemistry final, or coping with a difficult supervisor at work, or striving toward a particular career goal, or even something as small as recuperating from a nagging cough, didn't that involve you too? Didn't you think about her, even worry about her, and try to do all you could to help? If you could do nothing else, did you not try to comfort and encourage her?

As you began to move naturally into this position, you were preparing to take the role God designed for you in marriage. He intends for husbands to look out for their wives in every way, and He gave us the pattern in Jesus Christ's concern and active care over His people, the church. To love your wife responsibly means you communicate to her that she is important, and what is important to her is important to you. By word and by action, you say to her, "I understand. I respect you. I love you. Your concerns are my concerns. I want to take care of you. I want to treat you most tenderly and protect you and shelter you from anything that would hurt you."

In today's world, wives need more protection than ever. In two-thirds of American families, the women work full- or part-time. Nineteen million American mothers work, and it's estimated that within five years three-fourths of the *new mothers* in America will be working outside the home.[2] The husbands of these women have a serious responsibility to meet their wives' special needs.

If your wife works outside the home, always, but especially when you have small children, she needs your tenderest support. If you want to know how God sees her, consider Isaiah 40:11, "He (the Lord God) shall feed his flock like a shepherd; he shall gather the lambs with his arm, and carry them in his bosom, and *gently lead those that are with young*" (italics ours).

You can nurture your working wife by providing nonsexual physical attention—a supportive hug, a back massage, arms around her at night before she goes to sleep—and by guarding her health and her strength. Don't let her overdo. Remind her that she cannot be everything to everyone and help her arrange her schedule so that she has some time for herself.

Give her emotional support. Listen to her without offering quick advice—just listen with understanding and sympathy. Encourage her! Remember that as a woman she is much more apt to blame herself when things go wrong at work. Since she tends to be more subjective and sensitive in her dealings with supervisors and co-workers than you, she will probably suffer more acutely than you when things get out of order in her home—for a woman's house is an extension of herself, whether she has time to give to its care or not.

Do your share of the errands, home responsibilities, and child care—without leaving the impression you are doing it for her *as a favor*. This is not an act of nobility on your part; it's guarding the precious wife God gave to you. And, in simple fairness, if she is contributing to the family income, which is *your* God-given responsibility, then it's up to you to help on the homefront, which is *her* God-given responsibility.

To love your wife responsibly means nothing less than putting her ahead of yourself as you look out for her best interests and highest welfare.

This does not mean "lording it" over her and certainly it does not mean nagging. At a crowded driver's license bureau this week a husband was observed as he accompanied his wife while she obtained a license. Although potentially attractive, the wife appeared nervous and insecure. It was easy to understand why. Her husband watched her pose for her license photo in glum silence. Afterward he observed, "Your collar was all rumpled. It looked terrible. And why didn't you smile?" As they waited for the results, twice he loudly ordered her to "Quit picking at your face," while she wilted in embarrassment.

This husband apparently saw his wife as a second-rate person, not knowing he had set her in that mold by treating her in a second-rate manner. The principle is that the wife in many ways will be a reflection of her husband and his treatment of her. To put it in selfish terms: If you want to be married to a princess, treat your wife like one. To put it in biblical terms: Since the two of you are one in God's eyes, if you love yourself, you ought also to love the one who is a part of you. Do you love her as responsibly as you care for your own body? She needs this, and God counsels you to do it, even though it may go against the grain of your selfish tendencies.

Marriage demands more of us than any other human relationship and demands the most from the husband, who is to follow the example of Christ. He gave His very life for us that we might experience His love and then love Him in return. Just so, your wife needs you to give your love to her so that she can experience it and then love you in return. God designed her to be a *responder* to you; He designed you to be an *initiator*—to love *first and forever*.

2. LOVE HER WITH UNDERSTANDING AND HONOR

You will also need to love your wife with a three-part knowledge that (1) understands her personally (2) appreciates her inestimable value and (3) recognizes her position in God's sight.

This counsel comes from 1 Peter 3:7: "Husbands, likewise live with your wives in an understanding way, showing respect for the woman as you would a fragile vase, and as joint heirs of the grace of life. . ." (THE NEW TESTAMENT IN EVERYDAY ENGLISH).

Jay Adams comments,

Husbands are addressed directly, and commanded . . . to be careful and considerate about how they live with (their wives). They must stop living in ignorance of their wives' problems, desires, needs, longings, fears, etc. (as so many men do who have never bothered to try to come to an understanding of them), but literally, "according to knowledge"—in an understanding way.

The old cliche, "You'll never understand a woman," must be squelched. Husbands need to be told—as, indeed, Peter tells them—"There is one woman you must understand: your woman! God commands it."[2]

How does a man go about understanding his wife? First, by wanting to understand her so much he will give himself over to the adventure of knowing her. Second, by making a careful and loving study of her. One young husband describes how he spent time noticing everything about his bride—even the rhythm of her breathing. He discovered that when she was angry she began cleaning out closets and drawers; that when she was troubled, she stared out of windows. He knew what it meant when she looked down and did not meet his eyes. He came to understand what it signified when she turned her face against his shoulder. He observed her blushes, her passing moods, and her changing expressions. She came to realize that when he asked her, "What are you thinking?" he really wanted to know, because he longed to know her as deeply as possible. This young man literally "dwelt with her in knowledge."

Respect for your wife is the second gift of love based on knowledge. This respect calls for gentleness toward her. Peter explains to husbands that their wives are not inferior to them, but different. You need to understand that your wife is physically weaker and emotionally more sensitive and vulnerable, and so, must be handled with care. Jay Adams observes that many men treat their wives as they would an old tin garbage can, rather than as a fragile—and valuable—container, "a fragile vase, Ming dynasty!"[3]

We have been considering up until now New Testament counsel to husbands, but to learn how to apply this respect principle, we must turn to the Old Testament where we find the only book in the Bible devoted exclusively to love, sex, and marriage. The Song of Solomon reveals the pattern of married love as God designed it, gives a practical model for the love life of husband and wife, and guides us in living the principles in Ephesians 5 and 1 Peter 3:7. We suggest that you read this with your wife and make it a part of your own language of love.

In the opening of the Song of Soloman a king brings Shulamith, a chastely-reared country girl, to his palace as his bride and queen. Observe this bridegroom's gentle treatment of his wife and the great respect he shows her.

His love and approval was not just a private matter. The king showed publicly his adoration and respect for his wife. In the royal banqueting house, his banner over her was love. . . . It became obvious to everyone that Shulamith was the most important person in his kingdom—to be honored, respected, and protected in every way. He treated her like a queen, and that is what she became in truth. At the same time he privately loved her in such a way that she could finally give herself completely to him, withholding nothing of her trust, her thoughts, and her love.

Husband, how do you treat your wife publicly? Do you open doors for her . . . seat her at the table . . . hold her coat for her? These small courtesies give honor to the wife as the more delicate vessel. After all, your wife cannot *see* your mental attitude toward her. You must show it by simple actions that display your love and your care and protective concern for her well-being. Is your love a banner over her when other people are present? Do you often look at her? Respond to her glances? Listen to her? Make her feel she is the most important person in *your* kingdom?[4]

The word *respect* in 1 Peter 3:7 can also be translated *honor*. *The Expository Dictionary of New Testament Words* explains that this is "primarily a valuing." In this case it becomes a recognition of a wife's value and preciousness. Do you regard your wife as your treasure?

The third knowledge you must have is an understanding of God's spiritual assessment of your wife: She is a joint-heir with you of the free gift of eternal life. Although you have been given the privilege and responsibility of acting as God's representative in your home, never forget that your wife has an equal status before God and an equal reward to anticipate. Your roles are different, but you are spiritual equals. And if you forget this and dishonor your wife, Peter warns, you cannot expect God to honor your requests in prayer!

Husbands, in the same way be considerate as you live with your wives, and treat them with respect as the weaker partner and as heirs with you of the gracious gift of life, so that nothing will hinder your prayers (1 Peter 3:7 NIV).

3. LOVE HER CONSTRUCTIVELY

When, as a new Christian, Dr. Wheat set out to learn how to love his wife, he discovered this compelling truth: *Love is always doing the best for the object of one's love.*

If a husband follows this principle, he will love his wife constructively, just as Ephesians 5:29 counsels. To love a wife constructively means to nourish her—physically, emotionally, and spiritually—enabling her to mature and reach her God-designed potential. Consider these excerpts from four letters, each from a different woman, and each a heart cry from a wife who has not been nourished by her husband:

Wife A: "My husband is the breadwinner. I receive money for the food needs, but no money for my own personal needs or clothing. He seems to resent having to spend money on me. How do I handle this?"

Wife B: "I have to work, and I come home exhausted and feeling as though I need to be ministered to. Instead, I must always attend to my husband's needs and my children's needs. I don't know how to balance my life. Help!"

Wife C: "How should I react when my husband calls and says he will be late for dinner due to work and I don't believe he really needs to stay at work. I try very hard to make our home a pleasant place to be, but I feel he would rather be at work than home with me."

Wife D: "What part should I take when my husband, who's a Christian, does not lead in any of the spiritual areas of the family? The children long for their Daddy to lead them in devotions, and I need his leadership too."

Traditional marriage vows reflect this need for the wife's

nourishing. When a husband endows his spouse with all his worldly goods, the provision of all physical necessities is implied. And when he promises to take care of her "in sickness and in health," physical care is indicated. When he pledges to honor and cherish her, this refers to her mental and emotional well-being.

Ephesians 5:26–27 deals with the spiritual care of the wife. In comparing Christ and the church to husbands and their wives, Paul explains that Jesus gave himself to make his bride holy, set apart, cleansed by the Word of God, radiant, without stain or wrinkle or any other blemish. To apply this in your marriage, remember that you are God's representative to bless your wife and nurture her spiritually. You do this, primarily, by taking the lead in bringing the Word of God into every area of your thought and life. Let it speak to both of you and listen to its counsel. Did you know that the word *success* is used only once in the Bible? It appears only in correction with knowing and heeding the Scriptures:

> This book of the law shall not depart out of thy mouth; but thou shalt meditate therein day and night, that thou mayest observe to do according to all that is written therein: for then thou shalt make thy way prosperous and then thou shalt have good success (Josh. 1:8).

We have known couples who began, while dating, to complete their evenings together by reading Scripture and praying. One girl said, "If it were possible, I think I loved him more during those times than any other. He took charge. He was reading the Bible from Genesis to Revelation, so wherever he happened to be in it, he read those chapters aloud to me, his arm around me, sometimes our cheeks touching as he read. Then we would both pray. But he initiated it, and it convinced me even more that this was the husband for me!"

At our LOVE LIFE Marriage Seminars the longing most

frequently expressed by wives is that their husbands would become spiritual leaders in their households. Often, they say, "He will read the Bible with me if I ask him to. But I want him to take the lead!"

Their longing is God-implanted, for it is by His design. This way of nourishing will reap the most precious of fruit. Try it and watch your wife become more beautiful, with an inner beauty as well as an outward radiance and serenity.

4. LOVE HER BY CHERISHING HER

The Bible tells you in Ephesians 5 that your wife needs to be cherished by you. Cherish surely is one of the most beautiful words in the language of love. It bears several different meanings, each with a message for the husband who wants to know how to love his wife. Look at this list of meanings as a fragrant bouquet of actions, which will bless your wife.

Cherish means to take care of tenderly; to keep warm as birds cover their young with feathers; to protect as a hen shields her chicks from harm. Do you shelter your wife with tender care, warming her with your love? One bride described the way her husband cherishes her. "The most wonderful part of being married," she said, "is going to sleep on my husband's shoulder every night with his arm around me. I feel so safe . . . so loved."

Cherish also means to hold dear, to treat with affection. It comes from the same root word as *caress*. Your wife needs nonsexual caresses, cuddling, kisses, and hugs. She needs to hold hands with you. Concentrate with sensitivity on the wonderful experience of holding her hand. Tuck a kiss into the palm of her hand when you're leaving for the day. Cuddle her on your lap at the end of the day—not as a signal for sex, but just for cherishing.

Finally, cherish means to encourage or support. Let your wife know you value her opinions and enjoy communicating with her. Listen to her! Learn how to build her up. If you have learned to understand your wife, you will know almost immediately in what area she needs support and how to give it to her.

5. LOVE HER ROMANTICALLY

Your wife has a deep need to be loved romantically, as we described in chapter one. She needs you to have and to hold a vision of her truest self, to see through her flaws to the image of God in her, to perceive the beautiful person she is becoming, created and redeemed by God through Christ with an eternal identity.

Strangely enough, when lovers become husbands, they sometimes forget how to be romantic—the very thing their wives need and desire. If forgetful lovers could only realize that the sweet thrills of *being in love* provide an expectancy which literally transforms ordinary life. This line from an old book seems to describe what marriage is like when romantic love still flowers: *Our lives were so thronged with small beauties, it was as if we were children of the rainbow, dwelling always in the morning of the world.*

One woman wrote, "I need proof that there is something inherently lovable in me. Through my lover's eyes and words, pursuit or response, I see myself as I need to be seen. Some women writers nowadays scorn romantic love. But the stories of Cinderella, Sleeping Beauty, and Snow White are still locked within our collective memory. They do contain a truth at their heart: each woman needed the Prince's kiss, the Prince's choice, to be brought to fullness of life. God made me that way too."

The best way to learn to love your wife romantically is to study the Song of Solomon and absorb the ways he loved his bride. Note how he talked to her and about her; note his caresses, his love gifts, his occupation with her, his intense desire to know her better, to look into her eyes, to hear her voice.

6. LOVE HER REALISTICALLY

While this may sound like a contradiction, your wife needs to be loved realistically, as well as romantically. If she thinks you have idealized her, she will be afraid of disappointing you. No woman wants to live on a pedestal. Give your wife the security of knowing you see her as she is and that you love her with an unshakable love. When she feels at her very worst in appearance, or in self-image, or in mood or behavior, that's when she needs most to know you love her. So tell her . . . show her by comforting her . . . and don't forget the power of praise.

The husband/lover in the Song of Soloman gives husbands the pattern to follow in meeting this need in their wives. His bride, who was deeply tanned from working in the vineyards, felt inferior to the elegant, pampered, white-skinned women of the court. Her husband, understanding her feelings, skillfully and lovingly built up her self-image by praise. He sensitively praised her in the areas where she felt most insecure. He voiced his appreciation of her physical appearance and of her lovely character in specifics, not in vague generalities. He told her she was "altogether lovely." But he did not say this just when they were courting or on their wedding night. He continued to praise her even as their marriage matured.

Husband, your wife needs to know that you see her as she is, and think that she is beautiful—inside and out. This will actually produce a shining new loveliness to delight you. Wives who believe they are beautiful *are* beautiful.

As one wife told us, "This week I was really down. I'm struggling to lose fifteen pounds, and I hate my new haircut, and I have a cold. I'm tired and my eyes are red, and I feel like I can't do anything right. Do you know what my husband did? He put his arms around me, and looked at me very deeply, very searchingly, and then he said, 'I find you altogether lovely.' The way he said it, I knew he meant it. I honestly believe that moment has changed my whole life. I'll never forget it!''

7. LOVE HER SACRIFICIALLY

It is easy to define this as loving your wife enough to die for her. Some husbands do love their wives this much. But few will have to meet this particular test. Instead, the question is, do you love your wife enough to *live* for her? This, too, requires a sacrificial commitment.

One wife said wistfully, ''My husband is so good. I believe he would even give up his life without counting the cost to save me from harm. He would give his all for me. It's just that he won't share his all with me. I mean, he won't share himself and his life with me. I always feel a sense of distance—and it hurts.''

Dwight Small reminds us that caring is a sacred trust; we are ultimately accountable to God for the way we care for our mate. He asks several hard questions worth our careful consideration:

Am I willing to order all my values and activities around caring, making it the primary aim of my marriage and all else secondary?

Am I willing to accept the new demands and new disciplines that caring may impose upon me?

Am I willing to pay the ultimate price of caring: to make continual acts of self-relinquishment as caring shall require?[6]

He explains,

Caring has a way of ordering activities and values around itself; . . . Many things previously felt to be important will now fade in significance, and things related to caring will take on a new importance. What is found to be incompatible with caring, you must exclude; what is found to be irrelevant to caring, you must subordinate. In other words, you are to safeguard the conditions that make caring possible.

This is no easy task. It doesn't happen automatically. Rather, it requires conscious and continuous surveillance over all that touches your life. The more precious a relationship, the more it warrants safeguarding. So it is by the safeguards you employ to protect it and the sacrifices you make to sustain it that you show the worth of the relationship in your own value system. Caring partners will realistically count the cost and commit themselves to pay it.[7]

You will love your wife sacrificially when her happiness and well-being are more important to you than your own and when you are ready to give yourself, without counting the cost, for her highest welfare.

To love your wife as God designed becomes the challenge of a lifetime. This is one chapter we hope you will read and reread for the sake of your marriage. Every husband needs to keep these great principles of love in mind. Always remember that the God who commanded them will give you the strength, wisdom, and sensitivity to *live* them with your own beloved wife.

9

How to Love Your Husband: The Wife's Handbook

If the husband's responsibility can be summarized in one phrase: Love your wife! your calling as a wife can also be summed up in a few words: Respond to your husband!

As we discussed in the previous chapter, the biblical command "love your wife" comes highly charged with meaning. But when we search the Scriptures to find what the wife's response includes, we discover how all-encompassing and significant her part is.

Many girls marry without an understanding of their beautiful opportunity in the marriage partnership. For example, a wife complained recently, "I do love and respect my husband. And I appreciate all the help he gives me with our children and the house. But I get frustrated with him because he doesn't believe I care about him. He just can't seem to understand that I find it very hard to respond physically or even to show my approval verbally!"

Our counsel to her applies to every wife reading this chapter: You must remember there is only one way to convince your husband that you love him, and that is by your loving response—a response that he can see, hear, touch, feel, and enjoy on a daily basis, a response that includes the physical, but also touches every aspect of his life. This is your contribution to a love-filled, lasting marriage. Many wives who have enjoyed lifelong love affairs with their husbands say that this is their secret of success.

A husband simply delights in a responsive wife. And (although this is no excuse) he often looks elsewhere when he does not find it at home. As Gary Smalley warns,

A man's self-confidence is directly related to the way others respond to him. A man will tie his affection to those who respond to him and remove it from those who don't.[1]

Not only does your husband's self-confidence rest in your hands for safe keeping. The way you respond to him, even now at the beginning of marriage, will be a strong indication of the kind of life you will have together. It's no exaggeration to say that your response (or lack of it) will set the tone in your home, determine the quality of your relationship, and seriously affect—for good or ill—the outcome of your marriage. Because God designed you to be a responder to your husband's sacrificial, protective love, do not lose something infinitely valuable by ignoring this aspect of His plan.

Before we look at the biblical counsel for wives, we want you to consider two things. First, count the special abilities God has given you as a woman to fulfill your part. Unless you were taught unhealthy inhibitions in childhood, you probably enjoy using your natural skills to build loving relationships. You have an instinctive ability to love, to cuddle, to nurture, and an innate desire to give yourself to those you love. You are apt to be intuitive, affectionate, and person-centered. You most likely think in concrete, personal details rather than general ideas, and are more concerned with relevant facts than theoretical discussions. You find it easy to communicate intimately about feelings and perceive happenings below the layer of the obvious. You have, at least, potentially the gift of listening with your heart to the people you love.

Some of these abilities may, as yet, be undeveloped. Some may have been smothered by years of stress in the working world. A career wife once said, "It seems harder to be a woman these days. It's as though I need to be two very different people, all in a twenty-four hour period. I love my job, but I don't want to lose the qualities that make me special to my husband and children!"

In a study of the Type E woman, Harriet Braiker found that although a woman today lives under far greater work and achievement pressures than her forerunners, her defined role as principal nurturer and attender to the emotional needs of others has remained virtually unchanged.[2]

But no matter how demanding or inconvenient, most women do not want to give up this role or exchange their unique abilities for more masculine qualities. Dr. Braiker observes that

> while women want to succeed, need to succeed, few want to give up their cooperative natures in exchange for male competitiveness. While women yearn to be competent and independent, few would forfeit their parallel need to be loved and nurtured by a man; few women would trade their emotionality and need for intimacy for cold rationality and social withdrawal.[3]

She concludes that although women today want to participate in society in meaningful ways beyond their privilege of bearing babies and their responsibility of rearing and nurturing children, "for the most part, American women still want what they have always wanted—a husband and a family, or an enduring love relationship with a man."[4]

As we suggested to husbands in chapter eight, the man who wants to love and nurture his wife will protect her wife's emotional and physical well-being and help her to enjoy her chosen role in the home, even though she works

148

outside the home by necessity or by choice. No woman can expect to be everything to everyone, and the one who tries will soon find herself drained of the ability to respond to those who need her most. We see the dramatic cultural revolution in our country, which has swept more than nineteen million wives and mothers into the labor force, as another opportunity for husbands to learn to love and protect their wives under changing conditions. The Bible speaks to all cultures and all times, and we can never say, "But this truth just doesn't apply anymore." The principle in every culture is that husbands are to love their wives as Christ loved the Church and that wives are to respond to their love.

Now we'd like you to think about ways you can respond to your husband. If you are newly-married you cannot yet know all he really needs and desires. But let's list some things almost every husband wants from his wife.

Your husband needs you to respond to him physically in lovemaking. He needs your emotional response in nurturing him. He needs you to respond in practical ways in helping to establish and maintain your home and family (which may well include financial assistance). Your husband also wants your encouragement in all the activities he is interested in or feels called to do. Perhaps most of all, he needs you to demonstrate consistently your genuine respect and admiration for him as a man who is handling the challenges of life and handling them well.

These are the husband's needs and desires. If it sounds like too much, please remember this: What the husband hungers for almost exactly parallels the Creator's guidelines to the wife.

The Bible communicates these guidelines to us by several different methods. They appear as statement of fact, as example, and as commandment. While four or five earthly authors wrote them down over a period of about 1,500 years, we can see an amazing unity in their message—another proof that they were authored by one mind, the mind of God, for our blessing and happiness in marriage.

Our search of the Scriptures to discover how wives can best love their husbands will take us from the creation account of Genesis to the wisdom of Proverbs; through romantic, scented gardens in the Song of Solomon into the New Testament where the letters to Timothy and Titus offer a wonderfully concrete and concise statement of what the responsive wife *is* and *does*. We will conclude in the epistles of Ephesians and 1 Peter, which reveal two things every wife needs to know: 1) the best gift she can give her husband; and 2) what will make her most beautiful in his eyes.

Here's what to look for on this guided tour. You will find that everything a wife can do for her husband comes under these three ways of loving: A wife loves her husband and meets his needs by (1) helping him; (2) responding to him emotionally and physically; and (3) respecting him.

As you relate to him day by day, you will be meeting (or ignoring) his needs in these areas. In the hectic arena of daily life, nothing falls neatly into categories, of course, so these ways of loving him will all be intermingled, but it will help you to think of them separately, to be reminded of what he needs, and to analyze how well you are doing in the challenge of loving your husband.

IN GENESIS: HIS HELPER

We begin in the Book of Beginnings, which tells us why God created woman. She was made to complement man because he was lonely and incomplete. She perfected him, making him whole and complete. Her first descriptive title was *helper*.

And the Lord God said, It is not good that the man should be alone; I will make him an help meet for him. And out of the ground the Lord God formed every beast of the field, and every fowl of the air; and brought them unto Adam to see what he would call them: and whatsoever Adam called every living creature, that was the name thereof. And Adam gave names to all the cattle, and to the fowl of the air, and to every beast of the field; but for Adam there was not found an help meet for him. And the Lord God caused a deep sleep to fall upon Adam, and he slept: and he took one of his ribs, and closed up the flesh instead thereof; and the rib, which the Lord God had taken from, made he a woman, and brought her unto the man (Gen. 2: 18–22).

Picture Adam in a perfect environment—but alone. He had the fellowship of God and the company of birds and animals, plus a fascinating work of observing, categorizing, and naming all the living creatures. But because he was alone, this was *not good*. So the Creator provided a perfect solution: He made another creature, like the man, and yet wondrously unlike him. She was taken from him; yet she perfected him. God made her totally suitable for him spiritually, intellectually, emotionally, and physically. When Adam first saw her, his response was one of delight and a sense of belonging. He recognized that she was "the help meet for him" (KJV), "The helper suitable for him" (NIV).

Before the Fall we can be sure the woman joyously responded to her husband/lover and helped him gladly. Today women sometimes picture their title "helper" as a subordinate position, one a servant or child might fill. This is far from accurate! In the Bible's original language, the word *helper* refers to a beneficial relationship in which one person aids or supports another as a friend and ally. Exactly the same Hebrew word is used for God Himself in several of the Psalms. For instance, Psalm 46:1 calls God our *helper*—"a very present *help* in trouble." Or Psalm 70:5, "But I am poor and needy: make haste unto me, O God: thou art my *help* and my deliverer. . . ." Or Psalm

115:9, "O Israel, trust thou in the Lord: he is their *help* and their shield."

One wife told us how secure her husband made her feel when he sat close to her, touching her hand or putting his arm lightly around her. When she thanked him for "keeping in touch," he smiled at her. "Don't you know," he said, "that I am drawing strength from you?"

This illustrates a biblical principle you need to remember. While you will do many beneficial things for your husband in the course of a marriage, you can help him most of all by what you *are*. Your character is what really counts in strengthening him and completing him—even in managing your mutual affairs and rearing your children. Character, of course, will express itself in your actions. That's the only way others can see what you are on the inside. Our stopover in the Book of Proverbs will focus on the wife's character in her role as her husband's trusted partner. The next best way to help your husband is to relate to him as his encourager in everything he does (which may involve practical help as well as emotional support.) Your help in consoling him when things do not go well is equally important.

Psychiatrist Paul Tournier explains how a man needs his wife's consolation.

> One of the highest functions of a wife is to console her husband for all the blows he receives in life. Yet, in order to console, there is no need to say very much. It is enough to listen, to understand, to love. Look at that mother whose child runs crying to her knees. She utters no word, and yet in a moment the tears have disappeared, the child jumps down, smiles all over his face, and heads out into the world once more where he will receive new blows. In every man, even the most eminent and the apparently strongest, there remains something of the child who needs to be consoled.[5]

If you can keep in mind that a helper is a *friend and ally,* and always check your responses by this standard, you will become the helper God designed you to be. Your husband will perceive your help as a sign that you love him, and his reaction will be to love you even more. Helping means doing even the smallest thing for him in a cheerful, loving manner. It takes only a little effort to do the kind thing at just the right time.

IN PROVERBS: HIS TRUSTED PARTNER

We are going to look now at a passage of Scripture which offers so much to the woman who wants to learn how to love her husband that we are including it here—every word of it. We have added a title: *The Wife's Alphabet of Excellence.* since in the Hebrew language each of the twenty-two verses begins with a consecutive letter of the alphabet. In other words, it has been carefully thought out, and it can yield riches of wisdom to your life, if you will give yourself to it.

Please read it several times. See what these timeless principles have to say to you as a woman approaching the twenty-first century. Do more than read it. Absorb its message through the pores of your being until you can feel what it means to be your husband's trusted partner for a lifetime. Think about how you can become this kind of wife. Consider the long-term rewards.

The Wife's Alphabet of Excellence

A capable, intelligent and virtuous woman, who is he who can find her? She is far more precious that jewels, and her value is far above rubies or pearls.

The heart of her husband trusts in her confidently and relies on and believes in her safely; so that he has no lack of honest gain or need of dishonest spoil.

She will comfort, encourage and do him only good as long as there is life within her.

She seeks out the wool and flax and works with willing hands to develop it.

She is like the merchant ships loaded with foodstuffs, she rings her household's food from a far (country).

She rises while yet it is night and gets spiritual food for her household and assigns her maids their tasks.

She considers a new field before she buys or accepts it—expanding prudently (and not courting neglect of her present duties by assuming others). With her savings (of time and strength) she plants fruitful vines in her vineyard.

She girds herself with strength (spiritual, mental, and physical fitness for her God-given task) and makes her arms strong and firm.

She tastes and sees that her gain from work (with and for God) is good; her lamp goes not out; but it burns on continually through the night (of trouble, privation or sorrow, warning away fear, doubt and distrust).

She lays her hands to the spindle, and her hands hold the distaff.

She opens her hand to the poor; yes, she reaches out her filled hands to the needy (whether in body, mind or spirit).

She fears not the snow for her family, for all her household are doubly clothed in scarlet.

She makes herself coverlets, cushions and rugs of tapestry. Her clothing is of linen, pure white and fine, and of purple (such as that of which the clothing of the priests and the hallowed cloths of the temple are made).

Her husband is known in the city's gates, when he sits among the elders of the land.

She makes fine linen garments and leads others to buy them; she delivers to the merchants girdles (or sashes that free one for service).

Strength and dignity are her clothing and her position is strong and secure. She rejoices over the future—the latter day or time to come (knowing that she and her family are in readiness for it)!

She opens her mouth with skillful and godly Wisdom, and in her tongue is the law of kindness—giving counsel and instruction.

She looks well to how things go in her household, and the bread of idleness (gossip, discontent and self-pity) she will not eat.

Her children rise up and call her blessed (happy, fortunate and to be envied); and her husband boasts of and praises her, saying,

Many daughters have done virtuously, nobly and well (with the strength of character that is steadfast in goodness) but you excel them all.

Charm and grace are deceptive, and beauty is vain (because it is not lasting), but a woman who reverently and worshipfully fears the Lord, she shall be praised!

Give her of the fruit of her hands, and let her own works praise her in the gates of the city! (Proverbs 31:10–31 THE AMPLIFIED BIBLE).

At first reading we may think, "This lady was a doer!" Count the action verbs. At least twenty times we are told what she *does,* and the last verse assures us that her *works* bring her praise in the city. She's obviously a "liberated" woman, a woman of many parts who could fit well into our century. Today's career wife can respect this competent, creative, energetic businesswoman who managed to balance her life so that neither her work, nor her worship, nor her role as a woman was neglected.

What did she do for her husband? Well, she operated as his equal partner in a totally trustworthy manner. The word *willing* summed up her attitude toward her work and way of life. She managed their household well; she benefited the family financially by earning a good income through her creative endeavors; she honored her husband by her good standing in the community; she trained their children with watchful concern and supervised the servants, taking

155

responsibility for their needs; she helped the poor in the community. She also brought her husband credit by the appearance of the family, the well-kept furnishings of the home, and by her own regal appearance, clothed as she was, not only in fine white linen and purple, but in strength and dignity.

She looked good, and she *was* good! She maintained her honored position with a servant heart that could forget itself to help others. She spoke with wisdom and also with kindness. In the unexpected moment when the pressure was on, the "law of kindness" controlled her tongue. One gets the feeling that this wife met life with enthusiasm because she was ready for anything. She kept herself and her family in a state of preparedness. Today we could say, "she had it all together."

As for her relationship with her husband, we know he was proud of her; he knew how hard it is to find this kind of wife, and he valued her as "far more precious" than jewels. He had a confident trust in her and relied on her. He knew she would comfort him and encourage him and always do him good. He delighted in praising her and was ready to tell the world that she excelled over all other women, even the most virtuous of wives. He respected her. He honored her. And she dwelled in the sunlight of his praise and approval.

This woman could give most wives an inferiority complex! But a deeper look at this passage reveals something more than just positive actions and good deeds on display. This is not just the success story of a biblical superwoman intended to frustrate the ordinary wife who pours over *The Messies Manual,* valiantly trying to keep her husband happy, her children healthy, her home in order, while holding down a job and teaching Sunday School.

No, this Scripture has something powerful to teach about *character*. The message for wives is this: The most important thing a woman can do for the husband she loves is to develop strength of character by fearing and worshiping the Lord. A woman's relationship with the Lord produces the quality of life we read about here, the character and behavior that will honor her husband and bless their entire household.

A noble character . . . strength . . . dignity . . . wisdom . . . kindness. These most valuable characteristics can be yours if you desire them and seek them over the course of your lifetime. God is faithful to produce them in you if you will only cooperate with Him. Remember that the best way to begin is by drinking in the truth of the Scriptures. The wife of Proverbs 31 was able to become a beloved wife, an honored mother, a supervisor at home, a capable businesswoman, a friend to the needy, and a respected member of the community because her focus remained on the Lord and His power. She possessed spiritual beauty and grew more beautiful with the passing of time.

A young husband told us of an experience when he saw these qualities in his wife and how he fell in love with her in a deeper way. "We had had quite a misunderstanding," he said. "I had spoken words to her that wounded her. This was just minutes before people arrived at our home for a couples' Bible study. I knew how hurt she was. But I saw her rise above it and fasten her thoughts on the Word of God. I heard her share some beautiful truths that helped others. I watched her looking after our guests so kindly and graciously. Even when her eyes clouded momentarily and I knew she was remembering the hurt again, she went on. I saw the reality of her faith, and I knew, as never before, how fortunate I was to have a wife like her! I could hardly wait until I had the chance to be alone with her again and make things right—to ask her forgiveness and kiss away the hurt and tell her how precious she is to me."

Dr. Wheat says, "As an older husband, it means everything to me to know that I can count on my wife in all the difficulties of life, as well as the good times and the ordinary days. I can count on her integrity, her commitment, her wisdom, her kindness, her ability to cope, and her determination to do whatever it takes to help me and our household. I think of Proverbs 31 as the description of my own trusted partner, who is always there when needed.''

If you want to love your husband and make him grateful every day of his life he married you, then take the wife of Proverbs 31 as your inspiration and model.

IN THE SONG OF SOLOMON:
HIS DARLING, HIS LOVE

Is it possible to continue a passionate, romantic love affair with your husband long after the honeymoon? God has given us this beautiful little book on love and marriage, which answers, Yes!

Observe the example of Shulamith, whom we meet first as a girl being courted, then a radiant bride, and finally an experienced wife. Frequently, her husband called her his darling, his love—words that in the Hebrew language were used for physical expressions of romantic love—kisses and caresses. We would like you to see that this wife was adored by her husband because of her physical and emotional responsiveness to him.

If you would learn how to fuel the fires of an ongoing love affair with your husband, study her behavior and responses. Analyze them. You'll find that her husband's lovemaking thrilled her, and she let him know it! She thought about him with longing when he was not present, and she focused her eyes and conversation on him when they were together, complimenting his appearance, expressing appreciation for his skillful lovemaking, and always communicating her high respect for him as a man.

She desired his kisses, responded to his touch, and even danced for his pleasure. Near the close of the book, after

158

they were well beyond the newlywed stage, she promised him still more physical delights and made plans for their romantic times together.

The wife who wants to love her husband *will* respond to him physically and emotionally. For most men that's the *sine qua non* of marriage—the one essential element. Most men would not have married without the expectation of this on a continuing basis. Few women can imagine the pain Dr. Wheat sees when he counsels men who have been rejected physically by their wives. They've been turned down in the bedroom, pushed away in the kitchen when they seek a kiss, and given an indifferent shoulder in the TV room when they offer a caress. It's devastating to them.

A wife's failure to respond sends a clear signal to the husband. He will not feel loved unless you show him you desire physical affection from him. And you should know that your enthusiastic response to his passionate lovemaking is the ultimate pleasure for him. You have it in your power to seal your relationship by your ongoing response to him.

One husband explained, "I think of it as a bonding, almost like the bonding between a mother and a newborn. My wife's 'being there' for me, always responding emotionally to me with a smile and a hug and a sparkle in her eyes when I come home—that draws me to her like a magnet. This becomes a security link between us. It's one of the best things about marriage."

IN 1 TIMOTHY: THE RULER OF HIS HOUSEHOLD

I will therefore that the younger women marry, bear children, rule the house . . . (1 Tim. 5:14).

Here is another way to love your husband: by helping him to rear, control, train, and discipline his children, and to *rule* his household.

159

Since this comes as a surprise to some couples, let's look at this a bit closer. The word *rule* is a Greek word combining the ideas of house and master (*despotes*) and from which we derive our English word for tyrant: despot, an absolute ruler.

Various versions of the Bible translate this word either as "guide the house," "manage the house," or "run the household." Clearly, the wife owns the privilege and responsibility of managing and directing all household affairs. This does not mean she must do all the work alone or that she alone must make all the major decisions. But she is to plan, direct, and supervise in this area of their shared life. The household is her God-given province. The gracious, tactful, and considerate way in which a wife approaches her responsibility will be an accurate measure of her success. Proverbs warns that "the contentions of a wife are as a continual dropping (of water through a chink in the roof)" (19:13 THE AMPLIFIED BIBLE). "It is better to dwell in a corner of the housetop (on the flat oriental roof, exposed to all kinds of weather) than in a house shared with a nagging, quarrelsome and faultfinding woman" (21:9 THE AMPLIFIED BIBLE).

The Arabs stated this principle aptly in a proverb, which has become an inside joke for one family we know: "Three things make a house intolerable: *tak* (the rain leaking through), *nak* (a wife's nagging), and *bak* (bugs)."

We have already seen in the Book of Proverbs how the wife's management of the household can benefit her husband. Derek Kidner explains,

> The woman is the making or the undoing of her husband . . . his "crown"; or else "rottenness in his bones." . . . On her constructive womanly wisdom chiefly depends the family's stability, and if she happens to possess exceptional gifts she will have ample scope for them.[6]

Love your husband by managing the household. But be careful to do it with tact and grace.

IN TITUS: HIS LOVING WIFE

The old women . . . should be examples of the good life, so that the younger women may learn to love their husbands and their children, to be sensible and chaste, home-lovers, kind-hearted and willing to adapt themselves to their husbands—a good advertisement for the Christian faith (Titus 2:4, 5 PHILIPS).

At the beginning of this biblical tour, we suggested that wives need to love their husbands in three ways: by helping them, by responding to them emotionally/physically, and by respecting them. In these two verses, we find the whole package—a marvel of concise instruction.

First, on the list we find response: The young wife needs to learn to *love* her husband and children with an affectionate, responding love. It cannot be commanded, but it can be learned.

Second, we find help—helping her husband by what she does, which could be summed up in one word: homemaking. And, perhaps even more important, helping her husband by what she is. Three Greek words describe the character traits that are seen as top priority for the wife. Since all three words are words that have been borrowed for women's names—some wives have found this an easy way to keep their character goals in mind. For instance, to be a *Sophronia* is to be sensible and self-controlled, habitually governing yourself from within. It is a poise maintained with wisdom which keeps you from doing or saying foolish things on impulse, or letting some desire have power over you.

To be an *Agnes* is to share in God's purity, by keeping yourself away from the defilements of the world; to be chaste. It can mean avoiding crude talk, turning off

161

television shows which have the power to pollute the mind, and choosing your friends with care. It does not mean refraining from sexual pleasures with your husband. Remember that Shulamith, a passionate lover, was called "My dove" (my pure and innocent one) by her husband.

To be an *Agatha* is to be kindhearted—a term which implies action. You will be involved in all sorts of kindly activities for those you love.

Finally, the Scripture in Titus counsels wives to demonstrate respect for their husbands. We will look at this more closely on our next stop in Ephesians.

IN EPHESIANS: HIS ADAPTABLE WIFE

The best gift you can give your husband—that's the topic of this discussion. Unfortunately, it's a topic often misunderstood, so let's look at it in its scriptural context from the key passage in Ephesians.

> Be subject to one another out of reverence for Christ, the Messiah, the Anointed One. Wives, be subject—be submissive and adapt yourselves—to your own husbands as [a service] to the Lord. For the husband is head of the wife as Christ is the Head of the church, Himself the Savior of (His) body. As the church is subject to Christ, so let wives also be subject in everything to their husbands. Husband, love your wives, as Christ loved the church and gave Himself up for her. . . . Let each man of you (without exception) love his wife as (being in a sense) his very own self; and let the wife see that she respects and reverences her husband—that she notices him, regards him, honors him, prefers him, venerates and esteems him; and that she defers to him, praises him, and loves and admires him exceedingly (Ephes. 5:21–25, 33 THE AMPLIFIED BIBLE).

As we saw in chapter eight, a wife's rights are awesome. She has the *right* to her husband's complete nurturing, protection, and sacrificial love! God commands a husband to do everything for her highest good, even to die for her if necessary. God asks the wife to do only one thing for him and that is to give him the gift of submission: an attitude compounded of respect and her willing adaptation to him. It also includes, as we read in Ephesians 5:33 (THE AMPLIFIED BIBLE), the admiration, which a husband needs as much as his wife needs romantic attention.

In the context of the Scripture, it seems plain that both partners are to be submissive in their relationship out of reverence for Christ and as a service to the Lord. The wife's role is to adapt herself to her husband, demonstrating respect and obedience. The husband's role is to show submissiveness by his care and concern for his wife. Both are serving the Lord and building a harmonious partnership.

The wife is to be in submission because the husband is the head of the wife as Christ is the head of the Church. It would be ridiculous to think of the true Church exerting authority over Christ or announcing its independence to do its own thing.

Submission does not mean the wife is inferior. Or that the husband has any right to *demand* obedience from her, or to lord over her. Thus, we can only look at it as a gift, which a loving wife gives to her husband for her protection and their blessing. In doing this she enters into God's perfect design for their relationship.

If a wife does not trust and respect her husband, it is devastating both to him and the marriage. But if she is able to look at her husband with eyes of reverence, he becomes a king among men. They experience a two-way blessing: she gives him the position of respect and as he gives her the place of honor.

Gaye Wheat shared her thoughts on this attitude of submission in *Intended for Pleasure*. She said,

> We know we aren't perfect wives. And our husbands know it too. But it is possible to keep them so happy that they

think of us as perfect, because in the details which matter most to them, we have learned to please them! Now, I am not talking about devious dealings or cute manipulations designed to befuddle our husbands into adoring us. They are not that easily fooled. And, most importantly, there is a better way to please them—a way that God can honor, because it is rooted in the New Testament principle of servanthood: "Ourselves your servants for Jesus' sake" (2 Cor. 4:5).

Of course, this does not mean that we are to behave like menials around our husbands. To serve one's husband for Jesus' sake does not demand that one be servile and abject. . . . *It begins with the attitude of thinking about him, instead of being preoccupied with myself.* It includes looking for ways, all the time, to help him and please him. In the words of Proverbs 31, this kind of wife will do her husband "good and not evil, all the days of her life." The behavior that pleases him flows out of an inner attitude that I have already chosen for myself—the attitude that my husband is the king of my household and the king of my marriage. Next to the Lord, he is the one I want to please the most. He is my top priority, right after Christ. So it is my joy and privilege to treat my husband as my "lord." And here I am in good company, for Peter in his first epistle instructs the Christian wives to adapt themselves to their husbands . . . and he goes on to point to Sarah as a good example: "Even as Sarah obeyed Abraham, calling him lord . . ." (1 Peter 3:6).[7]

Then Gaye summed up the rewards of this attitude:

The more you please your husband, the more he is going to be eager to please you. The more he attempts to please you, the more you are going to be happy and satisfied, so even more you are going to try to do the things which make him happy. This is the glorious cycle of response which we could call a circle, for a circle never ends. Once we step into that circle of love, we will not want to move out, and although our husbands may still know our limitations only too well, they will feel that whatever we do is *all right*. We have proved ourselves to be just the right wives for them.[8]

IN 1 PETER: HIS BEAUTIFUL WIFE

We have toured the Bible in search of the Creator's guidelines for wives who want to know how to love their husbands according to His design. At this last stop, we will consider three important questions:

What does a wife do when her husband can't (or won't) love her the way God commanded in Ephesians 5?

What does a wife do when she feels no respect for her husband?

What makes a wife most beautiful in her husband's eyes?

Now to find God's answers, read these verses from 1 Peter. This passage follows a section written about the Lord Jesus Christ, who, when He was mistreated, "simply committed his cause to the One who judges fairly" (1 Peter 2:23 PHILIPS).

In the same spirit you married women should adapt yourselves to your husbands, so that even if they do not obey the Word of God they may be won to God without any word being spoken, simply by seeing the pure and reverent conduct of you, their wives. Your beauty should not be dependent on an elaborate coiffure, or on the wearing of jewelry or fine clothes, but on the inner personality—the unfading loveliness of a calm and gentle spirit, a thing very precious in the eyes of God. This was the beauty of the holy women of ancient times who trusted in God and were submissive to their husbands. Sarah, you will remember, obeyed Abraham and called him her lord. And you have become her true descendants today as long as you too live good lives and do not give way to hysterical fears (1 Peter 3:1–6 PHILIPS).

We have stressed the fact that you love your husband by responding to his love. We have explained that your gift of willing adaptation to him (the attitude of submission) should be your response to his sacrificial love for you. But what if your husband can't or won't love you the way Jesus Christ loved the church, either because he is an unbeliever or because he chooses to reject the way of love. What if you don't have any love to respond to? Or what if you can't feel any respect for your husband because he's not respectable?

The Bible has one comprehensive answer to these hard questions: In such situations, your husband cannot control your behavior. Live and relate to him in a manner that pleases God, and commit the results to Him—just as the Lord Jesus had to endure hard things, but committed it all to the Father who judges rightly. In other words, go on loving him in all the scriptural ways we have described in this chapter. Respond to the Lord's love by obeying Him in this manner, even if your husband offers little that you can positively respond to. This is a true saying: Living as a Christian does not depend on anyone else!

For example, if your husband is not a respectable man, you may not be able to *feel* respectful toward him, but God requires you to *show* him respect. The Greek word for "adapt," used in the opening of 1 Peter 3, literally means *to be under authority*.

As Jay Adams explains,

Christians must respect the uniform with which God clothed husbands, even if they poorly fit it. The respect is directed toward God and His authority, not fundamentally toward the man in whom it is invested. When a wife speaks disrespectfully toward her husband, she really speaks in a manner that disregards God. That is serious.[9]

At this point in the discussion several questions about submission usually come up. Let us share some principles with you.

1. God does not ask a woman to be submissive to all men

in general, only to her husband and as a means of functioning in an orderly way within the home.

2. God never gave a husband the authority to require his wife to sin. Do what your husband asks—as long as it does not involve sinning. He has no right to ask that of you.

3. Since obedience has to do with action, and respect, with attitude, it is possible for a wife to obey her husband, yet not respect him. Likewise, a wife can make a show of respect, but avoid doing what her husband asks. The absence of genuine respect is not submission.

The last question to consider is: What makes a wife beautiful in her husband's eyes? Women will pore over the latest *Vogue,* have their hair done, buy a new outfit, and their husbands will probably enjoy the results. Husbands appreciate every lovely detail of their wife's appearance. When Shulamith's husband praised her, he left out almost nothing!

And yet, God says there's another kind of beauty that counts for more, that never fades, that reaches into a husband's heart, and has the power to melt it. This beauty can be bought or developed by an application of new cosmetics. It begins on the inside—within the inner life one lives before God—and as it begins to shine forth, something happens on the outside. A man may not notice it at first. Like the dawn that comes so gradually, who can say when it first appeared?

Eventually the husband takes notice. His wife may not be harassing him anymore, nor complaining, nor nagging at him to change. She has become calm and gentle. She treats him with respect and shows a concern for his wishes. She meets his gruffest moments with a quiet spirit. There's a purity about her, a beauty which he may not understand, but he loves it, and he begins to look at her as if he has never seen her before. He watches her to see the source of this change. And the Scripture indicates there is the distinct possibility he may change too; that he may come to Christ because his wife has won him "without a word."

Hopefully, you and your husband are already one in Christ. But even if he already loves you according to God's design, you can delight him and bless his life by developing your inner beauty. Jay Adams, commenting on this passage in 1 Peter, gives you this recipe:

> (Outer) beauty is artificial; it is added to the person. (Inner beauty) is genuine because it is the result of a change in the person herself. Adornment must be inward; the inner person of the heart must become beautiful in order to please God and to be winning. This hidden person, when so transformed, will become visible.

> Women who try to hold husbands or win husbands only by making themselves outwardly attractive misunderstand the fact that husbands really want a woman who is *herself* attractive within. Respect and obedience that issue in lasting values . . . such as a gentleness and quietness are *most* alluring and winsome. Wives who carp and criticize, who whine and whinny, who yell and scream, who argue and act stubbornly fail to exhibit this inner beauty. The gentle and quiet spirit (spirit here means *attitude* and *approach*) attracts; other attitudes and approaches repel.[10]

One more way to love your husband: by becoming beautiful on the inside for him!

10

"Forever"

He has made everything beautiful in its time; He also has planted eternity in men's heart and mind. . . .

Eccles. 3:11a Amplified

When God gives us something beautiful to enjoy, He gives us the desire to enjoy it forever! He has planted the fact of eternity in our minds, and the longings of our hearts reflect it. When, as lovers, we say "forever," we mean that we choose to be together "for time without end." And yet we realize that time must end for every living thing. What happens then? Does this mean the end of our love and the oneness we have shared? Will we never be together again? Or, if we meet in heaven, will it be only in passing? Will we be separate again, the process working backward: one becoming two?

It's a good idea to confront these questions early in your marriage, because the conclusions you reach will affect the way you live. We encourage you to develop an eternal perspective of love and marriage based on the truth. The Lord Jesus Christ said in His prayer before going to the cross, "Thy word is truth" (John 17:17). Not all of our questions will be answered, but the Scriptures provide all the truth we need on this earth, and the truth never changes. The answers we have to share with you in this chapter are what we believe the Scriptures teach or suggest concerning love and marriage in heaven.

First, we can be sure that there will be no marriages in heaven. The Lord Jesus, answering the Sadducees, said, "Ye do err, not knowing the scriptures, nor the power of God. In the resurrection they neither marry, nor are given in marriage, but are like the angels of God in heaven" (Matt. 22:29–30). Why? Because God has the power to raise the dead in such a manner that marriage is no longer needed.

God designed marriage for our blessing and well-being on this earth, but in heaven it has been replaced by something even better. Notice that we will not become angels, but we will become *like* angels in several respects: We will not marry; we will have immortal bodies; and we will be occupied with the glory of God.

Here are seven reasons why marriage is not needed in heaven

No Death; No Need for Reproduction

1. Our resurrection bodies will be immortal. Mortality will be swallowed up by life (2 Cor. 5:4), and believers will never again be able to die. In the same moment that their bodies become immortal, they also become incorruptible, or immune to change and decay. Since there will be no death in heaven, there will be no need to reproduce and rear children. (See 1 Cor. 15:42–57.)

No Need to Be Healed of Loneliness

2. Marriage will no longer be needed to heal mankind's loneliness, for there will be no loneliness in heaven. The Scripture says, "In thy presence is fullness of joy; at thy right hand there are pleasures as for evermore" (Ps. 16:11).

We Will Find Our Completion in Christ

3. Marriage was designed to bring completion to man and woman, as the two became one, but in heaven we will experience our completeness in Christ, and will be satisfied. The Scripture says, "For in Him dwelleth all the fullness of the Godhead bodily. And ye are complete in Him . . ." (Col. 2:9, 10a).

No Symbols: The Real Thing

4. There will be no need to picture the relationship of Jesus Christ and His church to a lost world through the symbolism of marriage. We will have the real thing at the "wedding of all weddings" when the church, the Bride of Christ, is married to the Lamb. (See Rev. 19:6–9.)

No Need for Protection in a Perfect World

5. Our love needs the protection of marriage (the house of love) on earth, but in heaven we will dwell in an ideal environment. The security of permanent commitment will be unnecessary in "a world perfect at last." (See Rev. 21:3–5.)

All Relationships Will Be Important in Heaven

6. It has been suggested that in heaven everyone will love everyone else with the intensity reserved now for two people who fall in love. The night before Jesus went to the cross, He told his disciples,

A new commandment I give unto you, that ye love one another; as I have loved you, that ye love one another. By this shall all know that ye are my disciples, if ye have love one to another (John 13:34–35).

From this time forth, love became the signature and insignia of all who believe in the Lord Jesus Christ. What is commanded on earth "comes naturally" in heaven among

171

immortal beings dwelling always in the glory of God—the God who Himself is Love. We can imagine that, as the air we breathe on this earth, so love will be the atmosphere of heaven.

Rodney Clapp suggests that

> At the resurrection, *all* relationships will be taken up to such a high level that the exclusivenss of marriage will not be a factor in heaven as it is on earth. It is not that in heaven marriage will be less. Rather, all relationships . . . will be infinitely more joyful than we can now imagine. . . .
>
> Imagine being "in love" 24 hours a day, seven days a week, and "in love" not simply with one person, but with everyone you pass on the street. . . . Only resurrected creatures will be strong enough to endure the weight— indeed, to enjoy it and see in each person a unique aspect of God's beauty.[1]

We Will Concentrate on God, Not Each Other

7. In heaven we will be involved with God's glory, even as the angels are. We will no longer be occupied, as we are now, with our marriage partner's needs amid the cares of this world; our lives will center around fellowship with God. (See Rev. 22:1–5.)

But what will happen to our love in heaven? Many couples ask this question after they find there will be no marriage in heaven. True, their union is housed in the public, legal, sacred commitment of marriage, but that's not all of it. In the process of living out their commitment, their relationship has become a living entity of love. They want to know what will happen to this. Although Scripture has told us very little on the subject, we can draw these conclusions.

First, love is the one thing that will last. It's the only thing we can take to heaven with us. Marriage as an institution is superfluous in heaven, but love is not. We can be sure that not one iota of the love, which we have felt and shared and demonstrated will ever be lost. If our love has been centered in God's love, it will grow and abound in the ages to come.

Then, too, we know that God's love is always personal and specific, "not a vague, diffused good-will towards everyone in general and nobody in particular."[2] Because New Testament love involves people and relationships, we can be sure that love will not be a vague and lonely ideal in heaven, anymore than it is on this earth. And if we have individuals to love and to love us there, we can feel confident that our earthly loved ones will be a part of it. If they are in heaven, we look forward to sweet fellowship with them as we adore our Lord God together.

We need to remember that we don't know all the good that God has planned for us. Jesus' answer to the Sadducees concerning marriage in heaven was not a complete discussion of the subject, but a concise response to an insincere question. He did not address the subject so important to us: the eternal relationship of those who are married in this life. We have no way of knowing if a special bond will exist in heaven between those who were husband and wife on earth. Although we cannot have the same relationship which we had on earth, and even though our lives will be too full and complete to miss it, it's difficult to imagine heaven without some closeness with those we have loved best on earth. We believe that we can trust His great lovingkindness to arrange all things for our joy in that day.

When we think of our love in heaven, it teaches us valuable lessons for our time together on earth.

Lessons in Loving

1. Gaining an eternal perspective on our love relationship can be very helpful. It reminds us, first of all, that our love

affair is not the highest good, the chief end of life. God is greater!

2. We see that our love for one another is everlasting only if its source is God Himself. All that we can offer apart from Him is mere passion, lust, infatuation, or sentimentality. We find that we don't even know how to love one another fully unless we have loved God first.

3. We discover that if we try to keep our love separate from God—jealously guarding our relationship, even from the Lover of our souls—our love will turn into something else. As C. S. Lewis wrote in *The Great Divorce,*

No natural feelings are high or low, holy or unholy, in themselves. They are all holy when God's hand is on the rein. They all go bad when they set up on their own and make themselves into false gods.[3]

4. We realize that no earthly love, no matter how wonderful and intimate and beautiful, can replace our need for closeness to God. He has created us so that there is a place within which can be satisfied only by intimate fellowship with Him. In the shelter of His love, our love for one another can safely grow and flower until it is transformed by heaven into something even more wonderful.

How To Make Your Marriage Beautiful In Its Time

We have only two more things to share with you, and they relate to your handling of time and eternity. Your love affair began in delight: now, to learn how to value time and prepare for eternity is the apex of wisdom that will bless you forever.

First, the matter of time. "Marriage is the greatest institution ever invented," a woman said, looking back on forty-six years with her husband. *"It means you are the most important person in the world for somebody else!"*[4]

Have you discovered that yet in your marriage? The lady was absolutely right. But for her, it was already over. Like her, we all have a limited amount of time in the classroom of love with our marriage partner. It may be forty-six years or even sixty. It may be much less. Whatever, our time is short, indeed, to love one another with the exclusive, intimate love that belongs only to earthly marriage.

When you come to the reality of this fact, it can well change the way you look at time . . . and love . . . and the miracle of ordinary life with one another.

In the Pulitzer Prize-winning drama, *Our Town,* Emily, a young wife of 26 who has died in childbirth, is allowed to revisit an ordinary day from her past. But she is warned,

"At least choose an unimportant day. Choose the least important day in your life. It will be important enough."

She begins reliving her twelfth birthday, but soon she cries,

"I can't. I can't go on. It goes so fast. We don't have time to look at one another. . . . I didn't realize. So all that was going on and we never noticed. . . ."

Another character comments from the grave,

"Yes . . . that's what it was to be alive. To move about in a cloud of ignorance; to go up and down trampling on the feelings of those about you. To spend and waste time as though you had a million years. To be always at the mercy of one self-centered passion, or another. . . ."

But it is Emily's question which echoes in the heart: "Do any human beings ever realize life while they live it?" She is told, "No. (*Pause.*) The saints and poets, maybe—they do some."[5]

Yes, the saints—Christians who are the sons and daughters of the God who inhabits eternity (Isa. 57:15) and created time (Gen. 1)—do possess the spiritual capacity to appreciate the miracle of life on this earth, and to value every moment of loving as a gift from our Father. But if we have it, we must choose to learn how to use it. As the old hymn warns, "See how time flies, the time that for loving and praising was given!⁶

James Dobson tells of a trip he and his family made in 1977 to Kansas City, Missouri, to visit his parents. As they drove to the airport when the visit was over, he asked his father to pray for their family. He said he would never forget his father's words, for it was their last prayer together:

And Lord, we want to thank you for the fellowship and love that we feel for each other today. This has been such a special time for us with Jim and Shirley and their children. But Heavenly Father, we are keenly aware that the joy that is ours today is a temporal pleasure. Our lives will not always be this stable and secure. Change is inevitable and it will come to us, too. We will accept it when it comes, of course, but we give you praise for the happiness and warmth that has been ours these past few days. We have had more than our share of the good things, and we thank you for your love. Amen.⁷

Dr. Dobson says that eleven years later, his dad's final prayer still rings in his mind:

"Thank you, God, for what we have . . . which we know we cannot keep." I wish every newlywed couple could capture that incredible concept. If we only realize how brief is our time on this earth, then most of the irritants and frustrations which drive us apart would seem terribly insignificant and petty. We have but one short life to live, yet we contaminate it with bickering and insults and angry words.⁸

Here are seven ways to value time and bless your marriage.

1. Thank God for the daily miracle of time. Arnold Bennett has called it

the inexplicable raw material of everything . . . You wake up in the morning, and lo! your purse is magically filled with

24 hours of the unmanufactured tissue of your life, the most precious of possessions.[9]

2. So live and so love your partner as though it were your last day to enjoy the gift of time together.

3. Ask God what He wants to do with your marriage in the time you have. Share the vision and fulfill it together.

4. Practice, every day, becoming more at home with one another—mutually adapting, mutually accepting.

5. Learn to value the miracle of ordinary days of living together. Ask God to open your eyes, your ears, your mind, your heart, and all your senses to the wonder of it.

6. Beware of wasting your time with self-centered passions, bickering, power plays, unkind words, idle self-pity, petty disputes.

7. Remember what is most important. Henry Drummond says,

> We know but little now about the conditions of the life that is to come. But what is certain is that love must last. God, the Eternal God, is love. Covet, therefore, that everlasting gift. . . . You will give yourselves to many things; give yourself first to love. Hold things in their proportion. *Hold things in their proportion.*[10]

How To Prepare Now For Eternity

God has placed eternity in our minds and hearts because we are eternal beings. Our human soul—that part of us which makes each of us a unique and distinctive individual—will live forever. It's a fact. Granted, it's a truth that troubles some people. They would prefer to think that they could do whatever they please during their lifetime and afterward go to sleep, never to awaken again.

But, no. Apart from the unmistakable evidence of Scripture, most people also know in their hearts that while their body will wear out, their soul—their being—will never die. We have no choice in this: we *will* exist forever.

But here's the point that some people miss to their eternal grief: We do have a choice concerning *where* we spend eternity and *how*. If we refuse to make a choice and "just let it all happen," that becomes a choice too, and we must live with the results.

Either we will enjoy eternal life in heaven where Jesus Christ went to prepare a place for us, or we will endure everlasting unhappiness and misery, separated from God and love and all that makes life beautiful, not for just a time, but through all eternity.

What is eternity? "Infinite duration without any beginning, end, or limit—an ever-abiding present."[11] What will it mean to spend eternity in heaven? Think of living forever in the vigor of your strength without the uncertainties of childhood, the trials of adolescence, or the frailties of old age. Picture inhabiting a beautiful present without yesterday's regrets or tomorrow's fears. Think of life without death or pain or sorrow. Picture the beauty and freedom and joy that can be yours in heaven. As wonderful as all that sounds, there will be much more which we cannot even imagine now. We are incapable of comprehending it, and we do not possess the language to describe it. We do have this: a sure promise which goes into effect even before we get to heaven, "Eye hath not seen, nor ear heard, neither have entered into the heart of man, the things which God hath prepared for them that love Him" (1 Cor. 2:9).

All these glorious things which God has prepared for us come wrapped in one package labeled *eternal life.* And the best part is that we can begin to enjoy eternal life immediately. It can be a permanent possession, a present experience; we don't have to wait until our earthly body wears out to receive it. Note the present tense of these Scriptures:

He that believeth on the Son hath everlasting life . . . (John 3:36).

He that heareth my Word, and believeth on Him that sent me, hath everlasting life . . . (John 5:24).

He that hath the Son hath life . . . (1 John 5:12).

The other side of this truth is just as true. If eternal life is present tense for some people, so is God's judgment for others. If we do not possess eternal life, we are under God's judgment, already condemned—even before our earthly bodies succumb to physical death. No one is in a neutral state!

God made His choice when He sent His Son to die in our place for our sins. He has provided the way out for us—- the way to be saved from the condemnation of sin and the sentence of death which already hangs over us. Now the choice is ours. The Lord Jesus says,

. . . the Son of Man must be lifted up, (on the cross) that everyone who believes in him may have eternal life. For God so loved the world that he gave his one and only Son, that whoever believes in him shall not perish but have eternal life. For God did not send his Son into the world to condemn the world, but to save the world through him. Whoever believes in him is not condemned, but whoever does not believe stands condemned already because he has not believed (and trusted) in the name of God's one and only Son. This is the verdict: Light has come into the world, but men loved darkness instead of light because their deeds were evil (John 3:14–19 NIV).

And John the Baptist adds his testimony,

The Father loves the Son and has placed everything in his hands. Whoever believes in the Son has eternal life, but whoever rejects the Son will not see life, for God's wrath remains on him (John 3:35–36 NIV).

Again, Jesus speaks,

179

I tell you the truth, whoever hears my word and believes him who sent me has eternal life and will not be condemned; he has crossed over from death to life (John 5:24 NIV).

The Apostle John explains our condition and our choice:

And this is the testimony: God has given us eternal life, and this life is in his Son. He who has the Son has life; he who does not have the Son of God does not have life (1 John 5:11–12 NIV).

It's plain that the only wise way to prepare for eternity is to obtain *eternal life.* What is it? The life of Christ within you. You do not receive it by joining a church or being baptized or by living a good life. All those things result from possessing eternal life.

You can only receive Jesus Christ by believing on the power of His Name to save you. Here, according to the Scriptures, is what happened on your behalf, and what you need to believe by faith in order to be saved and receive eternal life:

1. The Lord Jesus Christ at a specific moment in history died on the cross for our sins, bearing the sins of the whole world. Through that mighty act, by paying the death penalty, He opened the way for all of our sins to be forgiven. In Jesus our past is pardoned, and our sins are forgotten as though they had been put in the depths of the deepest sea and remembered no more.

2. After dying on the cross, Jesus was buried. On the third day He arose again from the dead, demonstrating to all people for all time that He is God, with all power and authority and resources for the life of the person who believes on Him. It is written, "For as many as received Him, to them gave He the power to become the sons of God, even to them that believe on His name" (John 1:12).

3. Redemption in Christ Jesus does more than pardon our sins. Forgiveness covers the past, but when we believe on the Lord Jesus Christ, receiving Him by faith, God not

only forgives our sins and redeems us: We also become sons of God, partakers of divine nature, and possessors of eternal life. We are taken into the family of God, and thereafter God deals with us as children.

J. I. Packer explains,

What is a Christian? The question can be answered in many ways, but the richest answer I know is that a Christian is one who has God for his father.

But cannot this be said of every man, Christian or not? Emphatically no! The idea that all men are children of God is not found in the Bible anywhere. The Old Testament shows God as the Father, not of all men, but of His own people, the seed of Abraham. 'Israel is my son, even my firstborn: and I say unto thee, let my son go . . . ' (Exod. 4:22f.) The New Testament has a world vision, but it too shows God as the Father, not of all men, but of those who, knowing themselves to be sinners, put their trust in the Lord Jesus Christ as their divine sin-bearer and master, and so become Abraham's spiritual seed. 'Ye are all sons of God, through faith, in Christ Jesus . . . ye are one man in Christ Jesus. And if ye are Christ's, then are ye Abraham's seed' (Gal. 3:26 ff.). Sonship to God is not, therefore, a universal status upon which everyone enters by natural birth, but a supernatural gift which one receives through receiving Jesus. 'No man cometh unto the Father'—in other words, is acknowledged by God as a son—'but by me' (John 14:6). The gift of sonship to God becomes ours, not through being born, but through being born again. . . .[12]

The human race is made up of two kinds of people—those who are alive unto God, and those who are already dead in their sins. There is no middle ground: Believers possess eternal life; unbelievers are, even now, under the condemnation and wrath of God.

Do you know your own identity as a child of God who can call God your Father? Do you know that you possess the life of Jesus Christ within you because you have already received Him and believed on His name? Are you confident of your destiny when you leave this life?

If your answers to the above questions are "no's" or if you are just not sure, here is a prayer which you may want to follow in expressing your faith in Jesus Christ as your Savior:

Heavenly Father, I know that I am a sinner and cannot do anything to save myself. I do believe that Jesus Christ died on the cross, shedding His blood as full payment for my sins—past, present, and future—and that He rose from the dead, demonstrating that He is God.

As best I know how, I am believing in Him, putting all my trust in Jesus Christ as my personal Savior, as my only hope for salvation and eternal life.

Right now I receive Jesus Christ into my life, I thank You for saving me as You promised, and I ask that you will give me increasing faith and wisdom as I study and believe your Word.

I ask this in the name of the Lord Jesus Christ. Amen.

After this, let all the good things begin! Now you can begin to discover the riches of eternal life, with God as your own Father. To write about those riches would require another book, but to sum it up in a few words: You will live the rest of your life and on through eternity, knowing that God is *for* you. You belong to His family for now and forever, and He will never leave you nor forsake you. *You belong!*

What, then, shall we say in response to this? If God is for us, who can be against us? He who did not spare his own Son, but gave him up for us all—how will he not also, along with him, graciously give us all things? Who will bring any charge against those whom God has chosen? It is God who justifies. Who is he that condemns? Christ Jesus, who died—more than that, who was raised to life—is at the right hand of God and is also interceding for us. Who shall separate us from the love of Christ? Shall trouble or hardship or persecution or famine or nakedness or danger or sword? . . . . No, in all these things we are more than conquerors through him who loved us. For I am convinced that neither death nor life, neither angels nor demons, neither the present nor the future, nor any powers, neither height nor depth, nor anything else in all creation, will be able to separate us from the love of God that is in Christ Jesus our Lord (Rom. 8:31–25, 37–39 NIV).

Here are seven ways to prepare for eternity.

1. Trust in Jesus Christ as your Savior, if you have not already done so, and receive the gift of eternal life.

2. Set yourself on the eternal adventure of experiencing what it means to belong to God's family through Jesus Christ.

3. Become actively involved in a Bible-teaching church. God has designed the local church to be the bulwark and support of His truth in your life; a means of spiritual growth; and a stabilizing factor as you establish your own family unit.

4. Commit yourselves as one to love and serve the Lord Jesus Christ all the days of your life.

5. Continue to grow in His love through Bible study, prayer, and obedience in all He shows you.

6. Bless each other with His love, drawing on His power and resources to be the husband or wife you were meant to be.

7. Look forward to being together . . . "forever"!

Notes

Introduction

[1] Marcia Lasswell, "Illusions Regarding Marital Happiness," *Medical Aspects of Human Sexuality* (February 1985): 154.

[2] Paul Tournier, *To Understand Each Other* (Richmond, Virginia: John Knox Press, 1967), 30.

Chapter 1

[1] Robert Frost, "The Figure a Poem Makes," *Collected Poems,* 1939. Quoted in *A Little Treasury of Modern Poetry* (New York: Charles Scribner's Sons, 1950), 798.

[2] C. S. Lewis, *George MacDonald: An Anthology* (London: Geoffrey Bles, 1946), 123.

[3] C. S. Lewis, *A Grief Observed* (New York: The Seabury Press, 1961), 13.

[4] Maggie Scarf, *Intimate Partners* (New York: Random House, 1987), 79.

[5] Judith Adams Perry, M.D., "Love Related to Marriage," *Medical Aspects of Human Sexuality* (June 1985): 243.

[6] John C. Haughey, S.J., *Should Anyone Ever Say Forever?* (Garden City, New York: Doubleday & Company, Inc., 1975), 62, 64.

Chapter 2

[1] Malachi Martin, *There Is Still Love* (New York: Macmillan Publishing Company, 1984), 207.

[2] Ed Wheat, M.D., and Gloria Okes Perkins, *LOVE LIFE* (Grand Rapids, Michigan: Zondervan Publishing House, 1980), 119.

[3] Jay E. Adams, *Marriage, Divorce & Remarriage in the Bible* (Grand Rapids: Baker Book House, 1980), 4.

Chapter 3

[1] James R. Mannes, "Love the One You're With," *Family Life Today* (March 1985): 41.

[2]David Hegner, *What Will Make My Marriage Work?* (Grand Rapids, Michigan: Radio Bible Class Publications), 8.

Chapter 4

[1]Jay E. Adams, *More Than Redemption* (Phillipsburg, New Jersey: Presbyterian and Reformed Publishing Co., 1979), 228.

[2]David Augsburger, *The Freedom of Forgiveness* (Chicago: Moody Press, 1970), 121.

[3]Ed Wheat, M.D., and Gloria Okes Perkins, *LOVE LIFE*, 199.

Chapter 5

[1]Domeena C. Renshaw, M.D. "Communication in Marriage," *Medical Aspects of Human Sexuality* (June 1983): 205.

[2]Martin Goldberg, M.D. "Commentary on Survey: Current Thinking on Why Some Marriages Fail," *Medical Aspects of Human Sexuality* (June 1982): 131.

[3]Renshaw, 205.

[4]Anthony Pietropinto, M.D. "Commentary on Survey: Distress Signals in Marriage" *Medical Aspects of Human Sexuality* (April 1984): 87.

[5]Judson J. Swihart, *Communicating in Marriage* (Downers Grove, Illinois: InterVarsity Press, 1981), 19–20.

[6]Carmen Lynch, MSW and Martin Blinder, M.D., "The Romantic Relationship" *Medical Aspects of Human Sexuality* (May 1983): 155.

[7]Donald G. Ellis, Ph.D., "Listening Creatively to One's Spouse," *Medical Aspects of Human Sexuality* (March 1983): 173.

[8]Czeslaw Milosz, *Selected Poems* (New York: The Ecco Press, 1980), 18.

[9]Barbara E. James, Ph.D., "The 'Silent Treatment' in Marriage," *Medical Aspects of Human Sexuality* (February 1983): 100.

[10]Ibid.

[11]Charles R. Swindoll, *Strike the Original Match* (Portland, Oregon: Multnomah Press, 1980), 102–111.

[12]Pietropinto, 88.

[13]Emily Dickinson, *The Complete Poems of Emily Dickinson,* ed. Thomas H. Johnson (Boston: Little, Brown and Company, 1890), 534–535.

[14]The Rev. Derek Kidner, M.A., *The Proverbs, An Introduction and Commentary* (London: The Tyndale Press, 1964; reprint ed., Downers Grove, Illinois: Inter-Varsity Press, 1972), 46–47.

[15]David Hellerstein, M.D., "Can TV Cause Divorce?" *TV Guide* (September 26, 1987): 4–7.

Notes

Chapter 6

[1] Harold Feldman and Andrea Parrot, eds., *Human Sexuality, Contemporary Controversies* (Beverly Hills, California: Sage Publications, 1984), 130–131.

[2] Dean Sherman, "Singles and Sex, Logical Loving Limits," *The Last Days Magazine* 9, no. 2 (1986): 30.

[3] Ed Wheat, M.D., and Gaye Wheat, *Intended for Pleasure* (Old Tappan, New Jersey: Revell, 1981), 236.

[4] S. Craig Glickman, *A Song for Lovers* (Downers Grove, Illinois: InterVarsity Press, 1976), 25.

[5] Ed Wheat, M.D., and Gloria Okes Perkins, *LOVE LIFE*, 76.

[6] Wheat, *Intended for Pleasure*, 214.

[7] Helen Singer Kaplan, M.D., Ph.D., *Disorders of Sexual Desire* (New York: Simon and Schuster, 1979), 61.

[8] Ibid.

[9] Steve Beauvais, "What Men Hate About the Women They Love," *Glamour* (April 1988): 315.

[10] Abigail Van Buren, *The Best of Dear Abby* (Boston: G. K. Hall & Co., 1982).

[11] Mike Mason, *The Mystery of Marriage* (Portland, Oregon: Multnomah Press, 1985), 127–128.

Chapter 8

[1] Gary Smalley with Steve Scott, *For Better or for Best* (Grand Rapids, Michigan: Zondervan Publishing House, 1982), 14–15.

[2] Harriet B. Braiker, Ph.D., *The Type E Woman* (New York: Dodd, Mead & Company, 1986), 2.

[3] Jay E. Adams, *Trust and Obey, A Practical Commentary on First Peter* (Grand Rapids, Michigan: Baker Book House, 1979), 100.

[4] Ibid., 101.

[5] Ed Wheat, M.D., and Gloria Okes Perkins, *LOVE LIFE*, 158–159.

[6] Dwight H. Small, *How Should I Love You?* (San Francisco: Harper & Row, Publishers, 1979), 191, 193, 194.

[7] Ibid., 191–192.

Chapter 9

[1] Gary Smalley with Steve Scott, *For Better or for Best*, 155–156.

[2] Harriet B. Braiker, Ph.D., *The Type E Woman*, 141.

[3] Ibid., 2.

[4] Ibid., 4.

[5] Paul Tournier, *To Understand Each Other*, 23.

[6] The Rev. Derek Kidner, M.A., *The Proverbs, An Introduction and Commentary* (London: The Tyndale Press, 1964; reprint ed., Downers Grove, Illinois: InterVarsity Press, 1972), 50.

[7] Ed Wheat, M.D., and Gaye Wheat, *Intended for Pleasure, 143–144.*

[8] Ibid.

[9] Jay E. Adams, *Trust and Obey, A Practical Commentary on First Peter*, 96.

[10] Ibid., 96–97.

Chapter 10

[1] Rodney Clapp, "What Hollywood Doesn't Know About Romantic Love," *Christianity Today* (February 3, 1984): 33.

[2] J. I. Packer, *Knowing God* (Downers Grove, Illinois: InterVarsity Press, 1973), 112.

[3] C. S. Lewis, *The Great Divorce (New York: The Macmillan Company, Macmillan Paperback, 1946), 93.

[4] Diana Trilling, quoted in *Cosmopolitan,* (March 1987): 229.

[5] Thornton Wilder, *Our Town, A Play in Three Acts*(New York: Harper & Row, Publishers, 1957), from Act III.

[6] Frederick William Faber, "The Remembrance of Mercy" in *The Christian Book of Mystical Verse* selected by A. W. Tozer (Harrisburg, Pennsylvania: Christian Publications, Inc., 1963), 77.

[7] Dr. James C. Dobson, *Love for a Lifetime* (Portland, Oregon: Multnomah Press 1987), 115.

[8] Ibid., 116.

[9] Arnold Bennett, *How to Live on Twenty-Four Hours a Day,* a condensation in *Getting the Most Out of Life, an Anthology* (Pleasantville, New York: The Reader's Digest Association, Inc., 1948), 166.

[10] Henry Drummond, *The Greatest Thing in the World,* A Revell Inspirational Classic, (Westwood, New Jersey: Fleming H. Revell Company), 55.

[11] William Evans, *The Great Doctrines of the Bible,* Enlarged Edition (Chicago: Moody Press, 1974), 35.

[12] Packer, *Knowing God,* 181.

Recommended Cassettes

These may be obtained from your local Christian bookstore or ordered from Bible Believer's Cassettes Inc., 130 Spring St., Springdale, AR 72764. BBC, Inc. is the world's largest *free loan* library of Bible study cassettes with more than ten thousand different teaching cassettes for loan. More than one thousand of these are on marriage and the family. Write for further information.

Wheat, Ed. M.D. *Before the Wedding Night.* An exciting counseling series for the couple planning to be married. One of the world's recognized authorities on premarriage counseling provides the medical, emotional, and spiritual counsel every prospective bride and bridegroom need to hear. These cassettes are also widely used by counselors in working with troubled marriages. Three hours on two cassettes.

Wheat, Ed. M.D. *Love-Life for Every Married Couple.* Listening together to this two-cassette album will improve your understanding and verbal communication concerning your love relationship. Three hours of positive counsel to enhance your marriage.

Wheat, Ed. M.D. *Sex Techniques & Sex Problems in Marriage.* In the privacy of their homes, couples are benefiting from this helpful, frank but reverent discussion of sex technique and solutions to sexual problems. Combines timeless biblical principles with the latest medical findings and treatment of sexual dysfunctions. Unanimously acclaimed by Christian leaders. Three hours on casssette.

Recommended Videocassettes

These are available from *Scriptural Counsel* , 130 Spring St., Springdale AR 72764.

Wheat Ed., M.D., Fooshee, George, and Sanchez, George. *Foundations for a Successful Marriage*. This permanent videocassette resource addresses potential problem areas of sexual maladjustment, family finances, and emotional and spiritual communication. Three counseling sessions, each about 43 minutes.

Wheat Ed., M.D., and Wheat, Gaye. *The Love-Life Marriage Seminar*. The Wheat's popular Love-Life Seminar, professionally video-taped before an audience at Coral Ridge Church, Ft. Lauderdale, Fla. Includes a television interview with Dr. D. James Kennedy. Six and one-half hours on eight videocassettes.

We want to hear from you. Please send your comments about this book to us in care of the address below. Thank you.

GRAND RAPIDS, MICHIGAN 49530

www.zondervan.com